# Return to the Land

## An Ephraimite's Journey Home

by

**Ephraim Frank**

# Return to the Land

## An Ephraimite's Journey Home
by Ephraim Frank

Cover by John Diffenderfer, Lebanon, Tennessee.
Cover Background Map: 1581 German clover leaf style map showing Jerusalem as the center of the world.
© 2004, Key of David Publishing, Saint Cloud, FL.

Published by:
Key of David Publishing
PO Box 700217, Saint Cloud, FL 34770
1.407.344.7700
www.keyofdavidpublishing.com

Distributed by:
Messianic Israel Ministries
PO Box 3263, Lebanon TN 37088
1 800.829.8777
www.mim.net

Printed in the United States of America.
All quotations are used by permission.
Unless otherwise noted, Scripture quotations are from the *New American Standard Bible* (NASB), © 1960, 1977, the Lockman Foundation La Habra, CA, and *The International Inductive Study Bible*, Copyright 1992, 1993 Precept Ministries Harvest House Publishers, Eugene, Oregon 97402.
*New King James Verses* (NKJV) are from The New King James Version, copyright (c) 1982, Thomas Nelson, Inc. All rights reserved.

ISBN 1-886987-18-1

Ephraim—
Ephraim is the given name of Joseph's
second son.  It means "doubly fruitful."
The name was also used to describe the
Ten Tribes of the Northern Kingdom,
also known as the Kingdom of Israel.

Ephraimite —
A name used to describe those of the
Northern Kingdom of Israel
(as opposed to the
Southern Kingdom of Judah).
These Ten Tribes eventually lost their
identity some time after they were exiled by
the Assyrians around 722 BC.
It is a generic term for these Israelites, or
Hebrews, from the natural seed of Jacob,
specifically those referred to as the
"Ten Lost Tribes."
The name likewise is used to describe the
"companions" who sojourn with
those of Ephraim
(Genesis 41:52; 2 Kings 17:34;
1 Kings 12:21 Ezekiel 37:15-28).

"I have surely heard Ephraim grieving,
'You have chastised me, and I was
chastised, like an untrained calf;
bring me back that I may be restored,
for You are the Lord my God.
"For after I turned back, I repented; and
after I was instructed, I smote on my thigh;
I was ashamed and also humiliated
because I bore the reproach of my youth.'
"Is Ephraim My dear son?  Is he a
delightful child?  Indeed, as often as I have
spoken against him, I certainly still
remember him; therefore My heart yearns
for him; I will surely have mercy
on him, declares the Lord.
"Set up for yourself roadmarks, place for
yourself guideposts; direct your mind to
the highway, the way by which you went.
"Return, O virgin of Israel,
return to these your cities.
"How long will you go here and there,
O faithless daughter?
"For the Lord has created
a new thing in the earth..."
(Jeremiah 31:18-22).

# Acknowledgments and Dedication

Along the path of my life many people have given much of themselves to me. They have poured out their love, shared their wisdom, experience, and talents. Without them I could not have written this book.

To each and every one of them I am sincerely grateful. I could even have dedicated this book to many of them. I thank the God of Israel for putting them in my path, yet my deepest heart's desire, and surely theirs too, is to acknowledge and give honor to Him.

It is therefore to Him that I dedicate this book.

In the opening pages of my testimony, I quote a Scripture from one of my forefathers who knew by faith his Shepherd God. His words correspond perfectly with my testimony too, as I am a product, in this generation, of the faithfulness of this same covenant-keeping God, who has been fulfilling the blessings that our forefather conferred upon his son Joseph and his progeny. This is what the patriarch, Jacob, made a confession of while blessing his beloved son: "The God, before whom my fathers Abraham and Isaac walked, the God who has fed me all my life long to this day, the Angel who has redeemed me from all evil, bless the lads" (Genesis 48:15-16).

I pray, as did David, one of Israel's beloved kings: "Give ear, O Shepherd of Israel, You that leads Joseph like a flock; You that dwells between the cherubims, shine forth. Before Ephraim and Benjamin and Manasseh stir up Your strength, and come and save us. Turn us again, O God, and cause Your face to shine; and we shall be saved" (Psalm 80:1-3).

Ephraim Frank
Alfe-Menashe, Israel

# Contents

# Foreword

How many of us today consider, take to heart or think relevant a covenant that the Creator of the universe made with one man 4,000 years ago, a covenant replete with promises of blessings that would spread to all humanity and ultimately to the creation itself?

This covenant had to do with multiplying a race of people, whom the Holy One destined for faith and for a relationship with Himself. The seed promised to this one man was to become as numerous as the sands of the sea and the stars of heaven.

The records and account of this covenant relationship have been kept intact over the centuries by faithful scribes, men and women who believed the ancient writings to be the Word of the Creator.

Abraham, whose name means an exalted father of peoples, was the recipient of this covenant that God Himself was responsible to keep.

However, how is it possible to know if God was, or is, faithful to His Word in "real life," unless there we see a sudden realization by multitudes that they are these covenant people?

This book is the story of one such individual of the "seed of Abraham," whose life perhaps is not unlike many in this generation who are having a divine encounter with the God of Abraham.

The Prophet Jeremiah wrote down the words of the

Lord: "I will be the God of all the families of Israel and they shall be My people." And again, "Thus says the Lord, 'the people who survived the sword found grace in the wilderness; Israel when it went to find its rest...'"

Yes, it is only by His grace and faithfulness that at some point in history the creation would know that God is "the Elohim—the God—of Abraham, Isaac and Jacob."

I, being Jewish and a native of the Land of Israel, was brought up in school with the Tanach (Old Testament) and was taught the history of our people. Hence I knew that the Jewish people of today were not the only members of the family of Israel.

Since childhood I had been aware of the "ten lost tribes," but little did I know that I would marry one of those lost Israelites, after coming to realize that Yeshua (Jesus) is our Messiah, Son of the Most High God and descendant of King David, and that together my husband and my self would discover the great mystery that was hidden in the womb of the earth and begin to see it being unraveled in our day and age.

It is only an omnipotent Sovereign who is able to weave so miraculously into the smallest details of the lives of two human beings the greater strands of His overall eternal plan and create a "tapestry" out of those different fibers; small and great; ancient and new; individual and collective and make of them a union which reflects in some microscopic way the greater reality.

One of my favorite Scriptures in the New Covenant was spoken by a Jewish Believer and disciple of Yeshua, later to be one of the apostles:

"Therefore repent and return, so that your sins may be wiped away, in order that times of refreshing may come from the presence of the Lord and that He may send Yeshua (Jesus) the Messiah appointed for you, whom heaven must receive until the periods of restoration of all things about which God spoke by the mouth of His holy prophets from ancient times" (Act 3:19-21).

# Foreword

Ephraim and I can truly testify that in our lives we are experiencing those times of refreshing, as we are watching the restoration being enacted before our very eyes, while awaiting the return of our beloved King and Lord, Messiah Yeshua.

Rimona Frank

# Return to the Land

# Introduction

One day, as my daughter was working on a school project involving ancestry, she approached me for information about my side of the family. Prior to her inquiry, I had not given much thought to my biological heritage.

Her questions began to stir in my memory past events, and once I began to review the history of my father's fathers, I found myself walking out a most unexpected and enlightening journey.

Starting down this path led to a year and a half long period in which I wrote 33 letters describing past episodes in my life.

Those letters ultimately ended up in this book. It is my prayer that these writings will prove to be a source of encouragement and comfort to others who are walking out their faith in the Elohim (God) of Israel and in our Messiah Yeshua (Jesus).

Before we begin this journey into my past, I would like to quote one of our ancient forefathers. This is what Ya'acov (Jacob) had to say about his Elohim:

"The Elohim, before whom my fathers Avraham and Yitzchak walked, the Elohim who has shepherded me all my life long to this day, the Sent One who has redeemed me from all evil" (Genesis 48:15-16).

After reading these words I often prayed that by the end of my life, or even starting now, I would be able to express with absolute conviction this same confession of our forefather.

## Return to the Land

Perhaps the realization that Jacob had is one that has to keep growing within us. Nonetheless, I do hope that the underlying testimony of my entire life will be one that tells of the faithfulness of our Shepherd, the *Elohim* of *Avraham, Yitzchak*, and *Ya'acov*, the God of Abraham, Isaac, and Jacob.

When my life story is told, may it be one that gives good testimony about the covenant promises that the Shepherd God made to our forefathers, and to all the "seed" of Israel.

Ralph Ephraim Frank

## One

# In the Beginning

The full moon was still visible on that cold early morning in November 1944. My father was rushing my mother off to the hospital in his 1941 Pontiac. The time had come for this little seed of Abraham to be birthed into the family of Edward and Mildred Frank, residents of a small farming town in the State of Wisconsin, USA.

I was sprinkled (baptized) into a German Lutheran Church as an infant, and given the name Ralph Arnold Frank. Our provincial world was made up of small town folk, mostly farmers who reeked of the barnyards into which they put their hearts and souls. In the main, we were Lutherans and Republicans. The hard-working people I grew up among also hunted, fished, played sports, and of course, went to Sunday school, church, and "socials." The local tavern was one of the places where people from all walks of life would congregate, especially on Saturday nights. In this place there did not seem to be "any Jew or Gentile, slave or free," they were all "one in the spirits."

An old one room school that included all grades and one teacher was where I obtained my primary education (first eight years). There were seven of us in the class— one of the largest ever. Most of them, including the teacher, were related in some way.

## A Surprising Disclosure

One day at about the age of 12, I overheard a conversation between two fishermen who came to rent a boat from my father. One of them was the local mortician. He happened to be a very proud and strong German, with a name to match. The two were talking about my father's father, who owned the local tavern and was known for his friendly business manner, drinking habits, and card playing. The fisherman made a comment to the mortician about my grandfather being "Jewish." I knew that Grandpa and this "Morty" were friends, but what surprised me was the latter's outrageous response. I cannot repeat the curse words that spewed out of his mouth. "He is no #%*Jew!"

As I heard these words, I felt as though knives were being driven into my heart. This man's curses truly hurt me. I was especially fond of Grandpa, but as I began to think about it, I didn't remember him attending church very often. I thought it was because he worked late in the tavern on Saturday nights. Nonetheless, he did accompany Grandma on Christmas and Easter. My Grandma regularly attended church by herself and always had her prayer books and Bible in hand.

Grandpa Frank was a very enterprising guy. In the cold winter months he would buy raw furs from the Indians and local trappers and sell them to Jewish businessmen from Chicago or New York. In the summer he had a receiving station for sorting cucumbers, and of course, ran the tavern business year round.

My Grandpa had an older half brother who was the owner of the local store. Between the two of them they had a monopoly on the business in the area.

Every year we would have a big family reunion, but it was a reunion of my Grandma's side of the family (German Lutherans). These relatives had large families, and they all lived long lives.

I remember talk about the great-grandparents who were still living, yet what puzzled me was Grandpa's side of the family. Nothing much was ever mentioned about them. When later on my older sister did some research on the family, interesting facts came out of the closet. My great-grandfather and his first wife were Prussian Jews from the area of Posen, noted for its large Jewish community.

After the death of his first wife, Great-Grandpa remarried a non-Jewish woman. My grandfather was a product of that second marriage. Their last name was Franke, but later the family dropped the "e."

## So Quickly Lost

How quickly our family's Jewish identity was lost in just one or two generations!

A day would come when, based on my interest in, and involvement with "Israel," I would realize how much more true this would be of the nation of Israel during their course of more than 150 generations of wanderings in the "galut" (exile)!

I had always heard that many Jews were forced to convert to Catholicism, or that they chose to do so in order to preserve their lives in times of trouble and persecution, but what about those who concealed their identity by hiding among the Protestants and their various denominations? Were they still Jews?

I realized that, whether they assimilated in one religious institution or another, or even in another nation, the God of Israel had never lost sight of the children of His covenant people, nor of His ultimate intention for them.

My later studies on the subject would reveal that it was always His intention to hide Abraham's seed in such a manner that He could ultimately display and reveal the "works of His hand" before the entire creation:

"Therefore thus says the Lord, who redeemed Abraham, concerning the house of Jacob: Jacob shall not now be ashamed, nor shall his face now grow pale; but when he sees his children, the work of My hands, in his midst, they will hallow My name, and hallow the Holy One of Jacob, and fear the God of Israel.' These also who erred in spirit will come to understanding, and those who complained will learn doctrine" (Isaiah 29:22-24, NKJV).

The day would come when I would realize that everyone who has the faith of Abraham, also has a personal testimony (sometimes unbeknown to themselves) as one of the natural "seed" of Israel in this generation. And in Scripture we are exhorted not to conceal our true identity:

"Not to hide from our children, but to tell to the generation to come the praises of the Lord and His strength and His wonderful works that He has done. For He established a testimony in Jacob [you and me], and appointed a law in Israel, which He commanded our fathers, that they should make them known to their children; that the generation to come might know, the children yet to be born, that when they arise they will also declare, bear testimony to their children, and be encouraged to set their hope in God, and not forget the works of God..." (Psalm 78: 4-7, NKJV).

Hopefully, in the eyes of our next generation, our lives will be more than a mark on a tombstone in a cemetery.

While we are on the subject of cemeteries, I will never forget my grandfather's funeral...

He died when I was sixteen. The night before there had been a light freezing rain, but the next day was a bright, sunny, cold winter day; ice had covered everything. As we drove to the cemetery, it was as though the world was star-studded with rainbow-colored lights glistening off everything. I thought heaven had come to earth to pay a special tribute to a very special person —my Jewish Grandpa.

## Lutherans and Catholics

In Sunday school class, under the tutelage of my aunt, the lives of our Hebrew forefathers in Scripture were presented to my friends and me in pictures that were underlined with small captions.

One such picture that always caught my attention was that of Joseph. Sometimes I would just daydream into the pictures of the lad with the multicolored dress. The connectedness that I felt toward those "Old Testament stories" was beyond description. Although deep was certainly trying to call unto deep, at that time my life was totally taken up by being a "good American kid." And to me, this meant hard work, sports, and later on, beer parties.

During high school days my family had to deal with some tough ideological issues. I had a Catholic girl friend, and my older sister converted to Catholicism. At the time I thought our family was going to break up. My parents stopped talking to my sister and her fiancée, and they were very worried about me.

To get my father to attend my sister's wedding at the Catholic Church was no small "feat," as he swore that he would never set *his feet* in such a place. When he eventually did, he faced a memorable episode. Right in the middle of the High Mass and the ringing of the bells, the best man, who happened to be me, passed out!

After falling backwards down a couple of steps, I soon found myself sitting next to my dad in one of three big chairs in the front section of the church normally reserved only for visiting bishops.

So, here we were, seated in these places of honor during High Mass.

A Catholic friend of my father told him afterward that he had been a good Catholic for forty years, yet he had never once had an opportunity to sit on those chairs much less so during High Mass! But here my father, a

Lutheran (and a descendant of a Jew), comes into the church but once and right away takes up the Bishop's seat! No wonder God sits in the heavens and laughs.

After I graduated from high school, my parents immediately shipped me off to another state to a "good" Lutheran College.

Their plan succeeded, as my Catholic girl friend found another fellow. My heart was broken of course, but I seemed to find a certain freedom in not being tied down. Working, going to school, and keeping up with beer parties took up most of my time. In college, my best sleeping pill was reading the Bible. As a matter of fact, I was especially known for that particular trait. Although a mediocre student, I did graduate (by the grace of God) with a B.A. in Biology.

Ralph (Ephraim) Frank at age 2 ½ with his dog,
Skippy, and his beloved Grandpa Frank.

# Return to the Land

# Two

# Army Days

During my college years the United States was deeply entrenched in the Vietnam War. So as soon as I graduated, I was called into the army. Since I was a college grad, they gave me an option to attend officers training school, which I did. In just seventeen weeks I would come out supposedly ready to lead others into an insane battle in the jungles of a foreign land.

Hunting deer in the backwoods of a Wisconsin farm seemed much more natural to me. However, as "fate" would have it, or perhaps because I was one of those foretold by the Prophet Jeremiah, one who "survived the sword and [who] found grace in the wilderness" (Jeremiah 31:2), a few weeks before graduating from officers' school, I developed a painful cyst on my spine that put me into the hospital.

After recovery, I was given an option to start over again with another class, which would have entailed another three-year commitment, or to be a private and serve only another eighteen months. The latter sounded more appealing, so I filled out the "dream sheet" with others who were in the same situation. I chose to go to Germany, or to a camp somewhere close to Wisconsin. There were several soldiers from California in this group, and they all signed up to go to Fort Ord in Monterey Carmel, California. When the orders came back, they all went to Germany and I went to Fort Ord.

I arrived in San Francisco at midnight and waited in the cool fog with some others until 2:00 a.m., when the army bus finally came and we all got on.

Sitting next to me was Specialist Cahill. In the course of conversation he asked me what position I had been assigned to. I told him that I was going to be a drill sergeant in a training brigade for eight weeks, and then would be on my way to Fort Carson, Colorado to join the 7th Division—which ultimately would be going to Vietnam.

He asked me if I could type, and I said I could. He then told me that when processing-in later that day, I was to see a Sergeant Smith, to whom I was to report about my typing skills.

The next day we went through all the in-processing procedures. I finally had my orders, which read as originally planned. In the course of all of this I did not see Sergeant Smith, but just before we were to leave to go back to our living quarters, a big black Sergeant appeared on the scene.

Though somewhat intimidated by him, I was moved to overcome my shyness and to approach him with the message from Corporal Cahill. Before I could get the words out of my mouth, the big man grabbed the paper I was holding and said, "You can type?!"

I wasn't quite sure if this was a statement or a question, but he didn't bother waiting for my response. He told me that he needed someone urgently in his adjutant general branch for in-processing, and with the same breath instructed me to take these orders upstairs to Specialist Cahill.

The next day I started work at my new job as a clerk typist. Out of 50,000 military workers on that fort, what would have been the odds of sitting on the bus next to the Specialist who told me about this position?

Working in Army Administration had some advantages: I got to know many officers personally by using my family expertise: I tended bar for them at some of their parties.

A few months went by and finally orders came down from the Department of Army to go to Fort Carson and join up with the 7th Division.

Apparently no one informed the Pentagon that this little specialist first class had a change of jobs. So my friends, who worked in that section, told me that they had to report the mistake, and that it could take a while before the correction would be made.

At that time, I had only nine months left in the army, and anyone with less than six months to serve did not have to go to Vietnam. It took two months for the adjustment to be made and for orders to come with all the right information. I still had seven months. I did not know it then, but was later told that someone had forgotten to put my name on the roster for transfer and by the time the Department of Army caught the mistake, I had only four months remaining. So I was left to finish my tour of duty in California.

## A Change of Direction

Toward the end of my time in the army, the Holy One of Israel had another surprise waiting for me. I received a notice to go to a special meeting for high school dropouts. It had to do with an army-initiated program to help soldiers readjust to civilian life before being discharged. I did not qualify for the program, as I had a college degree, but a friend at work challenged me to go in spite of the obvious mistake.

A Lieutenant Colonel interviewed me about my interests. I told him that I had hoped to go into genetic research, specifically in the area of retardation.

He gave me a surprised look, as he thought I was a high school drop out, and he proceeded to question me about my education.

Upon finding out the facts, he immediately folded the paper he was taking notes on, and politely said that they had no such work, and that this program was not designed for personnel like me.

I was a little embarrassed for making an assumption, and returned to my workplace. However, about a week later I received a notice that the Colonel wanted to see me again.

To my surprise he told me that right after interviewing me he happened to run into a friend of his who had a retarded son. After talking to him about me, his friend put him in touch with the Director of Special Education of Monterey County. The County had a school for trainable mentally retarded on the base, and the message that was conveyed to me was that if I were interested in working there I had to meet the Director at the school.

The day after meeting with Dr. Bill, the Director of Special Education and School Staff, the Colonel called me in and said that I had been accepted into the program and could therefore embark working at that school.

Sgt. Smith was a little distraught at the thought of losing one of his staff, so he placed a condition on my leaving until a suitable replacement would be found.

This could have meant at least a month or more, but on the morrow the right person showed up at my desk, fresh from Vietnam!

The fellow was assigned to take my place, and because he already knew the job, I was at the school the following day.

After my discharge from the army, the county hired me on a full time basis.

It felt natural for me to work and play with multi-handicapped children. One of my first duties was to toilet-train the four and five year olds. On the third day at work, one of the children messed up her diaper and I was given the task of cleaning and changing her.

I gently took off the loaded diaper and placed it on the floor, right behind me. With my back to the door, I did not see one of the other little ones walk up and grab the dirty nappy and start swinging it around.

Needless to say, I had my baptism into Special Ed.

With that experience literally "behind me," I went back to school during the following three summers to obtain a degree in Special Education. Later on I became the Director of the County Child Development Center.

# Return to the Land

Ralph Frank
Carmel Beach, California

# Three

# Meeting the Master

As a young man in his twenties and living in California, my eyes were opened to a completely different way of life. I was hungry to experience the California life style and one of those pursuits was in the area of philosophy.

I had a strong desire to know and understand truth —thus the search for my "true identity" began. Just as the well known Greek philosopher had done in millennia past, I too posed the question: *"Who am I?"*

The Church did not seem to offer any answers to my questions, and as I previously mentioned, I found the Bible anything but interesting.

I was first presented with TM and the mystics, followed by clairvoyance, astrology, and Hatha Yoga. After a couple of years of dabbling in mainly Eastern philosophies, I was introduced by a friend named Bob to "Christ the great white light," and to the "great white brotherhoods" ("white" connoting purity and not racism).

This philosophy was based on the study of virtues and their application in daily life, and I sought to perfect the righteousness of my inner "christ," or "true self."

In this endeavor, I was assigned two spirit guides as teachers of the "enlightened" way.

The hidden secrets into the principles and laws that govern the universe were to be revealed to me through study and meditation. Application of those principles (some of them biblical), along with the virtues, was supposed to ultimately lead to high government positions in the New World Order like those of other "ascended masters," such as Jesus, Buddha, Mohammed, Moses, etc.

## Occult Involvement

For almost four years I walked as best as I was able in the way of the knowledge of "good," or "virtue," as taught through this philosophy—but the demand to walk out righteousness to its perfection always seemed to be out of reach. I kept failing to apply the principles in many of life's situations. I could identify with what one of the New Covenant Apostles wrote, "For the good that I will to do, I do not do; but the evil I will not to do, that I practice" (Romans 7:19, NKJV).

The deceiver is no fool; he knows that man cannot become "like God" in character, because there is an inherent flaw in his heart called "lust" or the "power of sin." However, to help seekers get around this hurdle, Satan built into their training process his doctrine of reincarnation.

Through this means of getting more than one chance, one could ultimately attain the next level of "godship" in one of the next "lives."

We were also told that really serious seekers of righteousness could invite the masters, or spirit guides, to enter their body during meditation in order to help work out this unattainable righteousness.

I was determined to succeed in this goal.

One night, I decided to overcome my fear and allow the "spirit guide" to take charge of my mind and physical body. About three months before this attempt at "astral exchange," my friend Bob went to his dentist, who happened to be what was called at the time a "Spirit-filled" Christian.

While Bob was lying back in the dentist chair, looking up at the ceiling, he read posters with the salvation message. That day he not only had a tooth filled, but was also saved and filled with the Holy Spirit.

I ran into him a couple of days later and noticed that he was "aglow." He gave me a big hug and started to share with me this Christian "charismatic stuff."

I thought he had gone "off his rocker." I couldn't believe that he would give up the philosophy and the New World Order for something so outdated and unenlightened. Needless to say, I did not have anything to do with him after that.

As for me, I was frustrated in not being able to make progress in what was supposed to be my "Christlike walk." I was even starting to entertain the idea of accepting homosexuality, which up till then had been abhorrent to me and definitely not a part of the "code of righteousness" I was trying to espouse.

With this struggle going on, in my desperation I was about to allow the ethereal guide to take over.

To prepare myself, I had memorized many of the teachings of the "Master" Jesus from the New Testament, along with many Psalms from the Old, as this was all part of the training of the "Western mindset."

The time had come for me to "meet the masters." However, before this special meeting, certain prayers of protection against demons were to be recited. Two of them were the Lord's Prayer and the Ninety-first Psalm.

After the prayers of preparation, I went, as usual, into meditation, sitting in a Yoga position on my bed.

Keeping very still, I soon entered the ethereal realm, losing all body consciousness.

Suddenly I felt as though something was jumping on the bed, but as I did not want to come out of this meditation session without succeeding in the "exchange," I just kept sitting with my eyes closed.

I had been warned about demons who try to distract

the process through fear tactics, so I did not relent.

## The True Master

All at once I saw a brilliant light, although my eyes were shut and it was dark in the room.

Immediately I snapped out of the state of oblivion that I was in. The peace in the room was absolutely incredible. Sitting and looking at my hands, I was thinking: "I'm still here!" At the same time I was amazed at the sudden peace which descended upon me. That night I went to bed with an awesome feeling that bordered on tranquility.

However, about 4:00 a.m. I woke up and was instantly alert. I had a strong urge to read the Bible. I opened it randomly to the first chapter of Romans and started reading:

"Although they knew God, they did not glorify Him as God, nor were thankful, but became futile in their thoughts, and their foolish hearts were darkened.

"Professing to be wise, they became fools, and changed the glory of the incorruptible God into an image made like corruptible man who exchanged the truth of God for the lie, and worshiped and served the creature rather than the Creator.

"Likewise also the men, leaving the natural use of the woman, burned in their lust for one another, men with men committing what is shameful, and even as they did not like to retain God in their knowledge, God gave them over to a debased mind, to do those things which are not fitting, being filled with all unrighteousness, sexual immorality, wickedness, covetousness, maliciousness; full of envy, murder, strife, deceit, evil-mindedness; they are whisperers, backbiters, haters of God, violent, proud, boasters, inventors of evil, disobedient to parents, undiscerning, untrustworthy, unloving, unforgiving, unmerciful; who, knowing the righteous judgment of

God, that those who practice such things are deserving of death, not only do the same but also approve of those who practice them" (Romans 1:21-32, NKJV).

## Self Realization

At that moment, in the early hours of the morning, I saw myself for who I really was. I fell on the floor in my room and wept bitterly for over an hour, repenting before a merciful God.

I did not go to work that day, but spent the entire morning reading the rest of the New Testament. I knew beyond a shadow of a doubt what the Apostle meant when he wrote "By Grace are you saved through faith... it is the power of God to salvation for everyone who believes, for the Jew first and also for the Greek. For in it the righteousness of God is revealed from faith to faith; as it is written, 'the righteous shall live by faith'" (Romans 1:16-17, NKJV).

## Saved by Grace

It was a beautiful spring afternoon, in the year of 1973, as I drove over to Bob's house. When I arrived, he had not yet come back from work, so I just went in and sat on the living room couch and waited.

When he returned, he was very surprised to see me sitting there. I jumped to my feet and hurriedly walked over to him. Grabbing him by his big shoulders, I began to shake him, crying: "Jesus is alive! Jesus is alive!"

Big tears began to roll down his cheeks, and as we embraced, we wept on each other's shoulders. Finally, half-crying and half-laughing, he asked me what had happened.

I told him of my intent to meet a "master" who was but an imposter, and that instead I had met "The Master." I had met the real Messiah.

In my excitement I continued to share with Bob what

had taken place the night before in my room.

With tears still streaming down his naturally rosy cheeks, he responded in a most amazing way:

"Last night at our prayer meeting the Holy Spirit came upon us mightily to bind those occult spirits that were working in your life."

We compared the times of the prayer and the time that I was blinded by that brilliant light that "popped" in my closed eyes like a flash from a camera, and there was no mistake; it was God's grace! Thus, another testimony of His mercy of saving a self-righteous wretch like me got under way.

Needless to say, my life was no longer the same. The Abrahamic seed of faith in me had at last sprouted and taken root.

"Has His mercy ceased forever? Has His promise failed forevermore? Has God forgotten to be gracious? Has He in anger shut up His tender mercies? And I said, 'this is my anguish!' But I will remember the years of the right hand of the Most High. I will remember the works The Lord; surely I will remember Your wonders of old. I will also meditate on all Your work, and talk of Your deeds. Your way, O God, is in the sanctuary; Who is so great a God as our God? You are the God who does wonders; You have declared Your strength among the peoples. You have with Your arm redeemed Your people, The sons of Jacob and Joseph" (Psalm 77:8-12).

## Charismatic Crisis

During the early seventies the grace of the Lord was moving through the denominational churches. The Holy Spirit was especially targeting the Catholics and as mentioned earlier, I had grown up in an environment that was prejudiced against Catholics. Yet, here I was in the midst of born-again, Spirit-filled Catholics who were hugging and loving me into a new life experience. I started to go to what were called "Life in the Spirit" seminars and to prayer meetings, where everyone sat in a circle with no apparent leader. The Spirit of God, and the reality of Yeshua (Jesus) dominated those meetings; with tongues, interpretations, words of knowledge, prophecies, short scriptural readings, testimonies, laying on of hands, praying for the sick and for the baptism of the Holy Spirit. Everyone, it seemed, participated.

There was nothing boring about these meetings. Especially exciting were the times of praise and worship. I was participating with others who brought their musical instruments to make a joyful noise. There was no formal organization and no set songs that we had to follow. The time just seemed to flow with the unity we all had in the Spirit.

It was a delight to get up in the morning and read the Bible, especially the Psalms. After about two years of this wonderful beginning, things started to change.

The group grew, and many more, especially Catholics from the local churches, joined in. The local priest began to show up at the meetings and he incorporated some parts of the Catholic Mass into our free expression. New "leadership" was chosen to help order the services, and it so happened that these leaders were involved in Transcendental Meditation.

After one of the meetings I had a blunt confrontation with the two of them. On the way home I was still angry, and at one point, I banged my fist on the steering wheel, shouting out to God: "How can this be?!"

The response, in a form of a question, came gently into my thoughts: "Who is under whose wing?"

I knew at that moment that God did not need me to defend Him. Soon I began to feel out of place, as Mother Mary and other typical Catholic traditions were being introduced. In one of the meetings I had a vision of a giant octopus with one of his sucker-bearing tentacles reaching out to surround and embrace the prayer group.

That was the last meeting I attended.

I next contemplated going back to the Lutheran church, which I eventually did, and my first Sunday there reminded me of old days. I sat like a bump on a log, while everything was being orchestrated and ordered. But what really threw me was the sermon on the virtues and their application to life in order to become more Christ-like.

I almost fell out of my pew! I thought I was back in the philosophy of the great brotherhoods. The sad thing is that their teachings were actually far superior to the sermon being promulgated that Sunday morning.

I thought to myself, "This pastor could use the teachings of the 'brotherhoods' to enhance his sermons."

I did not know exactly what to do. I was not inclined to go with the Catholics, but this seemed to be far worse. I stuck it out for a few months, thinking maybe some Lutherans would get turned on to this "Holy Spirit stuff."

But just the opposite happened. When the minister started preaching from the pulpit against the "Charismatic deception," I didn't feel welcome any more. But because I was one of their Sunday school teachers and the janitor at the church, I stayed on.

However, since some of my Catholic friends, who were in the original prayer circle also left, and joined with a small Episcopal Spirit-filled group, I did too.

## High Adventure

Again, I had a wonderful and enjoyable experience. In this group I met a middle-aged curly haired man named Norman. He always seemed to be led to exhort the brethren. Norman was a fiery and stocky guy with a reddish complexion. One of his favorite prophetic topics was Israel and the return of the Jews to their homeland.

Most of us, if not all, were not really interested, but he kept plugging away at us willy-nilly.

A new organization called the Full Gospel Business-men's Fellowship opened a chapter in Monterey at that time, and some of us men joined and helped establish the movement in our area. Norman was one of the leaders.

One of our first guest speakers, was Norman's friend, a fellow by the name of George Otis.

George shared his personal testimony interlaced with facts about Israel. A few weeks later, Norman came to the prayer group and proposed that we all go on a Holy Land tour with High Adventure Tours, hosted by George Otis and Pat Boone.

At first I was not interested. What's more, it seemed to me to be very expensive. But it wasn't long and most of my friends had signed up to go.

Never having been out of the United States, I thought that this would give me an opportunity to travel...

# Return to the Land

## Four

# A Life Changing Encounter

It was in late February 1976, when fifteen of us left Monterey for the High Adventure conference and a two-week excursion in the Holy Land. We were excited and it seemed that we sang from coast to coast.

We arrived in New York after six hours, only to wait another five or six hours before boarding the Israeli El Al Jumbo 747 aircraft. Security was very tight and being a first timer to all this I thought I was being unnecessarily harassed when interrogated, especially as a single guy.

They asked why I wanted to go to Israel. Once they questioned us, we were at last off into the black night skies.

The flight was quite uneventful and passed quickly. I was sitting next to the window when the announcement came to buckle up for landing. The sky was clear that winter day over the Mediterranean, and as I was looking out of the window to get a glimpse of the Land on the horizon, a Hebrew song came over the loudspeakers: *"Heveinu Shalom Aleichem..."*

They were singing, *"We bring you peace..."*

Many on board were singing along and at that moment, the aircraft banked and I saw the little strip of land on the horizon.

What happened to me next I will never forget

When I set eyes on the Land, everything inside of me cried out: *"I'm home, I'm home, I'm home!"*

Tears began to stream down and I thought to myself: "What is happening to me? Why am I crying and why do I feel that I'm home?" I tried to conceal my emotions from the others and put my hands in front of my face and just wept and wept.

I was amazed during those two weeks of touring, every place where we went in the Land seemed familiar to me, and the messages of the conference speakers went right to my heart. At one point, on the Mount of Olives, as we looked out over Jerusalem, the capital of Israel, my old friend Bob, who had gotten married and was standing there with his pregnant wife, looked at me. With his big finger pointing at the city sprawling below us, he said with a very definite prophetic tone: "The Lord just showed me your heart. Your wife is out there."

Being almost thirty-two years of age and still un-married, I thought I was going to be a "eunuch for the kingdom," but little did I know...

Being a product of American education there was something else that I did not know much about, and that was Jewish history. I was taught about Egypt, the Greeks and the Romans, but my learning was basically devoid of Old Testament history, except for those few Sunday School lessons on the Patriarchs when I was little. That made up all that I knew about this Land and its people.

Toward the end of the tour I was feeling as though my heart had been planted in the Land. As a matter of fact, I even changed the words of the popular song: "I left My Heart in San Francisco." I instead started singing: "I left my heart in Israel, high on a hill, it calls to me, where little donkey carts go skirting by the shops; the evening breeze will swiftly bring me back; as a matter of fact, my heart waits there in Israel..."

I don't remember the entire song, but this was all part of God's wonderful ordained plan for my life.

"For You formed my inward parts; You covered me in my mother's womb. I will praise You, for I am fearfully and wonderfully made; Marvelous are Your works, and that my soul knows very well. My frame was not hidden from You, when I was made in secret, and skillfully wrought in the lowest parts of the earth. Your eyes saw my substance, being yet unformed. And in Your book they all were written, the days fashioned for me, when as yet there were none of them. How precious also are Your thoughts to me, O God! How great is the sum of them! If I should count them, they would be more in number than the sand; When I awake, I am still with You" (Psalm 139:14-18, NKJV).

## An Awakening

My "high adventure" in the Land of Israel was indeed like a dream. It was a dream that I did not want to wake up from. Or was it the other way around: had I somehow been asleep up until that time, and suddenly an ancient awakening was happening deep in my soul?

"When the Lord turned again the captivity of Zion, we were like them that dream. Then was our mouth filled with laughter, and our tongue with singing: then said they among the nations, the Lord has done great things for them" (Psalm 126:1-2, NKJV).

The bus to Ben Gurion Airport carried many tired people. I could only sit there in silence and retrospect the intimate moments of this brief stay in the Land. We had been blessed and able to see:

Joseph's tomb in Shechem, the Mount of Blessing, Jacob's well, the Valley of Dothan, the Sea of Galilee, Nazareth, Capernaum, the Mount of Beatitudes, Massada, the Golan Heights and the Good Fence, the Dead Sea and Ein Gedi, Ellah Valley where David fought Goliath, Hebron and the graves of the Patriarchs, Bethlehem and Rachel's Tomb, Golgotha and the Garden Tomb, the Mount of Olives and Gethsemane, the Temple Mount and the Western Wall, the Holocaust Memorial,

Old and New Jerusalem and more.

On the other hand, the churches and cathedrals that we plodded through did not seem to leave the same lasting impression. The words of the guest speakers at the conference, which included a fiery prophetic speech by the caretaker of the Garden Tomb, Jan Willem Van der Hoeven, were still ringing in my ears.

Pat Boone sang one of his songs, taken from 2 Chronicles 7:14: "If My people who are called by My name will humble themselves, and pray and seek My face, and turn from their wicked ways, then I will hear from heaven, and will forgive their sin and heal their land" (NKJV).

All of the sights and sounds were racing through my memory like waves crashing against the seashore. By the time we reached the airport and were unloading the luggage, sadness had crept in like a fog on Monterey Bay at the end of a day.

The unexplainable melancholy I felt at the idea of leaving was obscuring my memories of the precious moments in the Land. It was leaving me with troubling thoughts: "Why am I leaving? I don't want to go!" People were talking to me, but I was oblivious.

There were about thirteen hundred people on the tour, so checking through the ticket counters presented some problems. At one point it was announced that there had been a mix-up. Because of over-booking some of us would have to stay behind and wait for another flight. This had been some of the best news I had heard all day long!

I quickly volunteered to allow others who had families, jobs, dogs, cats or anything else, to go ahead of me. Their reasons made no difference, all I wanted was to be able to stay, one way or another!

Those of us who remained behind received the news that there would be a flight ready in another five hours. Waiting on the floor of the departure lounge, time passed and still there was no sign of a flight, a fact which raised my hopes. Sadly though, after twelve hours it was time to board the plane for our trip back to New York.

## The Encounter

I was assigned an isle seat in the middle of the plane, next to an energetic teenager, who unbeknown to me was busy handing out Christian tracts to a group of Jewish businessmen from New York. These men had gone there to consider investments in the Land.

I wasn't paying much attention to the activities of this young lady, and found the seat next to her to be comfortable after twelve hours on a hard floor in the terminal.

My thoughts and emotions were still mixed, with questions and possible solutions to this dilemma of desiring to stay, in spite of the circumstances which were taking me in the opposite direction.

As the plane was taxing down the runway, I had to accept the fact that there was no turning back. Looking out a far window, the lights of Tel-Aviv were flickering in the background. I leaned back, loosened my seat belt and with a lump in my throat closed my eyes.

For the next half hour I was half awake and half asleep, as we settled into our cruising altitude. Suddenly I noticed a pair of pants, just to the right of my arm. As I lifted up my eyes I saw a man glaring down at me.

When our eyes met, he motioned me with a white knuckled fist and thumb to get up. I pointed to myself with hesitance, wondering if he really meant me. When there was no doubt that he did, I slowly rose to my feet, only to discover that my eyes were about level with the knot on his tie.

With teeth clenched and tight lips he uttered, as he looked to his right and then to his left: "Let's go to the back of the plane, I want to talk to you!"

He whirled and quickly walked toward the tail of the aircraft. I wanted to sit back down, as my knees were a little weak from the experience, but as I was about to do so, I found my legs moving in the direction of the big man, toward the back of the plane.

When I stood before him, feeling like a sheep led to the slaughter, I pushed myself behind the last two seats. Glancing to my right I saw the exit door, then to the left, where the toilet door was clearly seen.

I was wondering through which one of these doors he was going to toss me. All at once the man's nose came very close to mine, with only his pointing finger between us. His glare had turned to fierce anger (rage is probably a more appropriate description). For a second I thought I had detected fire in his eyes. He then began to speak to me very slowly. Through his clenched teeth and tight lips, making sure I didn't miss a single word he said, "Why is it that you Christians are always trying to proselytize and change we Jews, when all that we want to be is loved?'

My brain melted in my head, as there was no trace of a thought anywhere to be found. But then I heard myself say to him: "Could you forgive us for not understanding?"

He drew back, his countenance changed, and with tears in his eyes and also in mine we found ourselves embracing one another. He went back to his seat, and I went back to mine. I plopped myself down, and looking up at the light switches and air vents, I said almost audibly: "God, what was that all about? What do you mean by 'they should forgive us for not understanding'? What don't we understand?"

## What Don't We Understand?

I didn't get an answer in those moments, but was left to wonder whether that whole episode was real or not. I was too tired to think much of anything for the rest of the trip.

When I finally arrived back in Monterey, the lack of sleep and jet lag knocked me out for almost three days. Then I awoke one morning, at about four, and again posed my question to the Lord: *"Why must the Jewish people forgive us? What don't we understand?"*

In answer to my questions, thoughts came streaming into my mind that almost seemed audible:

"When My people see in and through you the love that manifested itself in all its fullness on Calvary, I will rent the veil and they will see me as their Lord and Messiah."

The thought offered a lot to chew on. The taste was bittersweet. I knew that I, along with probably most of the Church, still did not understand this providential relationship between the redeemed Gentiles and the Jews.

Trying to digest that statement, I reached over and opened my Bible. Again the book of Romans appeared in front me. As I read from it, I was overwhelmed. It left me wondering if I was not somehow a part of some great mystery that was about to unfold before the universe:

"And if some of the branches were broken off, and you, being a wild olive tree, were grafted in among them, and with them became a partaker of the root and fatness of the olive tree, do not boast against the branches. But if you do boast, remember that you do not support the root, but the root supports you. You will say then, 'Branches were broken off that I might be grafted in.' Well said. Because of unbelief they were broken off, and you stand by faith. Do not be haughty, but fear. For if God did not spare the natural branches, He may not spare you either.

"Therefore consider the goodness and severity of God: on those who fell, severity; but toward you, goodness, if you continue in His goodness. Otherwise you also will be cut off" (Romans 11:17-22, NKJV).

Branches of an olive tree. Some wild and some natural. Faith and unbelief. Goodness and severity.

Grafted in and cut off. What is this all about? What does all this have to do with my experience in Israel and the one on the flight back?

## The Mystery

"For I do not desire, brethren, that you should be ignorant of this mystery, lest you should be wise in your own opinion, that blindness in part has happened to Israel until the fullness of the Gentiles has come in. And so all Israel will be saved" (Romans 11:25-26, NKJV).

My mind, my emotions, were reeling in wonderment at a mystery that I knew I was meant to understand.

I could not escape the thought that what happened to me in Israel and this mystery were somehow connected. I thought maybe there were others who could tell me what this mystery was all about. So that morning I headed off to work with great expectations. I could not wait to talk to my believing friends, or to anyone else who could satisfy this thirst to know and understand the God of my salvation, the God of Israel.

Five

# Crossing Over

Using a Bible reading program before my first trip to Israel, I had read the Bible through from beginning to end. A couple of days after I had recovered from my Israel tour jet lag, I continued to repeat the program, taking up where I had left off before the trip.

On this particular morning I was to read Joshua chapters 1 and 2, along with Ezekiel 35 through 36. Again, one of those incredible, memorable happenings took place while I was reading this passage in Joshua:

"Arise, go over this Jordan, you and all this people, to the land which I am giving to them, the children of Israel...Be strong and of good courage, for to this people you shall divide as an inheritance the land which I swore to their fathers to give them. Only be strong and very courageous, that you may observe to do according to all the Torah which Moses My servant commanded you; do not turn from it to the right hand or to the left, that you may prosper wherever you go" (Joshua 1:2,6-7, NKJV).

Reading this, I shot out of bed and my feet went-a-dancing to a non-audible tune. My emotions were running high. I thought these were words given me from the Lord. I thought He was telling me that I was to pack my bags and head for the Jordan River.

I finally calmed down long enough to read the next installment, this time from Ezekiel.

"Thus says The Lord God to the mountains, the hills,

the rivers, the valleys, the desolate wastes, and the cities that have been forsaken, which became plunder and mockery to the rest of the nations all around... I have raised My hand in an oath that surely the nations that are around you shall bear their own shame. But you, O mountains of Israel, shall shoot forth your branches and yield your fruit to My people Israel, for they are about to come" (Ezekiel 36:4,6-8, NKJV).

That did it! This time I was weeping so hard that I couldn't even continue reading. I felt like a little lost child crying for his mommy, while at the same time wailing: "I want to go home! I want to go home!"

Later that morning I got into my little blue Datsun pickup truck, with its shell on the back, and started off for work. I couldn't wait to talk to someone about the things that were racing around inside my head.

On my way down the highway, I thought I would listen to a tape of some Scriptures that I usually carried round in the glove compartment of the truck. There were several to choose from, but not wanting to take my eyes off the road I settled for the one which my hand had randomly picked and slid it into the tape recorder. I thought perhaps the tape I had chosen would be the one with all the "begats," but to my surprise, out comes this prophecy:

"Thus says The Lord God to the mountains, the hills, the rivers, the valleys, the desolate wastes, and the cities that have been forsaken ...."

*The tape began with Ezekiel 36!*

I could not believe my ears. Needless to say I had to pull over and wait until my eyes stopped flooding with tears.

Over the next few months I tried sharing these Scriptures with others, and each time I made such an attempt I would choke up and not be able to finish reading.

## I'm Out of Here!

Several days after the "highway experience" some of us who had gone on the High Adventure tour met for a prayer meeting. One of the participants felt he had "a word" for me. He leafed through his Bible, then stopped, flipped back a page, looked down at the print for a moment, then looked up at me with a bewildered look on his face.

With his eyes focused on the open Bible in his lap, he finally read, in a very quiet but firm voice, the following:

*"Arise, go over this Jordan, you and all this people, to the land which I am giving to them— the children of Israel...Be strong and of good courage, for to this people you shall divide as an inheritance the land which I swore to their fathers to give them."*

I thought to myself, "That does it! I'm out of here!" At that moment a song by John Denver came to my mind: "All my bags are packed I'm ready to go, I'm standing here outside the door...cause I'm leaving on a jet plane, don't know when I'll be back again..."

"Amen!" I shouted. The brothers had to literally hold me down as I shared with them the Scriptures that I had received a couple of days before. They encouraged me not to be in a rush about something as crazy as leaving California and moving to Israel. I could not prove that I was Jewish anyway, so the chances of living there were next to nil.

## Dreams

During that year (1976) many other things occurred in my life; among them some significant dreams. In one dream I saw myself walking through rolling hills covered with long golden-colored grass. In front of me there was an old dilapidated barn, which I entered, coming out on the other side with a barrel full of different varieties of corn, wheat, barley etc.

Although the barrel was heavy, the trek was down a gently sloping hill, and the load did not seem to pose a problem.

Walking down this road I finally came to a small creek which was crystal clear and very shallow, but had a beautiful white sandy bottom. As I looked across, I saw the landscape; it was green and lush with fruit trees, shade trees, and farm animals grazing. Semitic looking men, women and children were relaxing and picnicking under the trees.

By this time, the barrel became heavy in my arms, and gathering a little more strength, I lifted it up and stepped into the creek, but lo and behold the bottom was like quicksand!

I dropped the barrel into the water and pulled myself back up on the bank, and I managed to pull the barrel out too. Now it was much heavier though, as the grain was mixed with sand and water.

Walking further down stream, I came to a place where it seemed possible to jump across. But as I glanced down at the water, it looked black, not because it was not clear, but because there was no bottom to be detected.

I got as close to the edge as I could, hoping I would be able to step across, while at the same time being aware that with the barrel in my arms both I and it could disappear into the deep.

I started to slip and as I was catching myself from falling, I dropped the barrel into the water.

I could see it disappear into the black hole.

Being somewhat scared, I turned to walk away, and at the same time looked down stream. I then noticed an earthen stone bridge that went across the creek.

With that, the dream ended.

When I awoke, the dream was very vivid in my mind. I prayed and asked for an interpretation, but the interpretation had to wait for hindsight. As it turned out, it was a prophetic dream about my future.

The golden grass and rolling barren hills represented my life in California. The dilapidated barn was my past, out of which I had emerged with education, talents, abilities, and experience all packed into this barrel that I thought would be useful to me in Israel. The water barrier clearly represented the Holy Spirit who was to govern my future. I was destined to make two attempts of my own volition to cross the creek, but the time would not be right for either attempt.

The opportunities would seem accomplishable, but once stepping into them the lesson would be made very apparent, and the Lord's purpose in each attempt would strip me of my reliance on my own talents and ambitions.

Then, after dealing with me and exposing my wrong motivations, I would be able to see the earthen stone bridge that He had already prepared for me. An *earthen* crossing meant that there would be nothing supernatural about my going over to Israel and living there; it would happen in the natural course of events.

At one point I asked the Lord what I would be doing over there. He answered quite simply that it would be something I had "never done before."

Shortly after this dream, I had another significant one, which was also fulfilled ultimately:

I saw myself standing in front of what looked like an outhouse, the kind that was used by the farmers in the "old days," before they had indoor plumbing.

The scene took place in an area that was surrounded by a cyclone fence with three strands of barbed wire around the top. I opened the door and walked inside, and almost immediately I started going down, as if in an elevator. It went down four stories, and on the way down I was losing my clothing. At one point I was concerned about my wallet, as it disappeared together with my clothes.

When I reached the bottom, I found myself dressed in a blue uniform, but to my amazement I was standing outside the little house, in the same area with the cyclone fences.

This time, though, I felt that someone was standing next to me. I did not see who it was, but just knew that there was someone there. We walked together out of an open gate, into what appeared to be clear blue skies. But as we walked I could still see the fence with the barbed wire on both sides. Just like the first dream, I was not given the interpretation until after its fulfillment.

"A man's heart plans his way, but the Lord directs his steps" (Proverbs. 16:9, NKJV).

## Six

# The Supernatural

In the summer of 1976, after my stirred up "Israel" emotions calmed down some, I encountered some "hair-raising" situations.

One such incident took place about two o'clock one morning, following an urgent phone call from a sister in the Lord who wanted me to come over right away to check on her husband who was "going crazy."

She had heard my testimony about my past involvement in the occult, and thought that perhaps I might have some insights into her husband's condition. He had been in Vietnam and afterwards got involved with the Masons. His behavior over the years had become more and more bizarre. He and I had a mutual friend, Tom, who came into the reality of the Spirit-filled life just a few weeks prior. I immediately contacted Tom and arranged to meet him at the couple's house.

Tom brought a friend with him who was a "borderline" Believer, but also an alcoholic. Upon arrival we could feel the cold chilling atmosphere of demonic presence in the house. Jan's husband was sprawled out in his easy chair, displaying obvious signs of having drunk one too many. Jan glanced at us with expectant faith, while I, for my part, was wondering what I was doing there in the first place. I certainly was not noted for any kind of ministry, except for music and periodically sharing a teaching in our small prayer group.

Jan then turned to us and said: "Here are his (Masonic) Bible and study books. What shall we do with them?"

Not thinking of their value, or maybe not thinking at all, I said, "Burn them in the fireplace."

What followed was something out of a horror movie. As the fire lapped up around these tossed objects, we heard screams from the fireplace. Jan's husband immediately sat up in the chair, with a noticeable change in his facial features. When we asked if we could pray for him he shook his head in the affirmative. I crouched down next to him and put my hand on his knee. Tom was standing behind the chair, with his friend behind him. Not being quite sure on how to pray, with a very quiet and timid voice I barely got out of my mouth, "In Jesus name."

All at once the fellow began to contort and squirm in his chair with both arms stretched out in front of him, wiggling like snakes. Tom's friend shot backwards about two paces. My eyes were about as big as pancakes, as I watched this man get set free from demonic possession. Later I found out that Tom's friend had also been set free from his problem with alcohol, and we didn't even pray for him! When we left the house, in the early hours of the morning, we were all amazed and humbled at the power of God's presence.

That night I learnt an invaluable lesson, as I witnessed God's Spirit move without our help. It was an incredible faith and confidence builder both in Yeshua and in His sovereignty.

Later on, and even to this very day, the effects of that night still linger as a testimony of Yeshua's presence in His people. But I also learnt not to try and reduce these experiences into formulae. This occurrence and its accompanying lesson were another preparatory step in the direction of the move to Israel. I began to learn what Paul meant when he quoted God saying: "I will have mercy on whom I will!" (Exodus 33:19; Romans 9:15).

## The Janitor Story

On the morning of Easter Sunday I went to a Lutheran church service. It was a little hard to get back into the traditional ways, but since being filled with the Spirit much of what was being read and expressed had become more meaningful and real to me.

During the service I noticed a young lady standing in the foyer of the church. She was very hesitant and seemed not to be able to decide whether to come in and sit down. After the service I went over to her and told her that Jesus loved her just as she was. At the time I did not realize how significant those words would be for her.

A month or so later I was walking out of the janitor's storage room at church and this same lady showed up, quite distraught. So it only seemed natural to pray with her to receive Messiah into her life. A couple of weeks later, at Bob's house, we prayed for her to receive the baptism in the Holy Spirit. The presence of the Lord in her turned her life around.

A month or so later Becky asked me if I wanted to help her drive a motor home from San Francisco to Ohio. I agreed, as it gave me an opportunity to visit my family in Wisconsin. We left San Francisco late Saturday afternoon and were on the road for about seven hours, when up in some very steep mountains terrain the motor suddenly made a couple of chugs and died.

I managed to get the huge vehicle off to the side of the road, where we just sat. The battery was getting so weak that it hardly turned the motor over. After about an hour I thought to myself that maybe we should pray. I did not have much confidence in God when it came to vehicles, my reason being that vehicles didn't have faith, so how could God fix them?! But I did get up enough nerve to invite Becky to pray with me.

We both prayed that God would send us help in the form of a person who knew something about mechanics. After the prayer we just sat there with not many cars in sight. Those that did pass didn't even slow up. As Becky was a very new Believer, I was getting more and more embarrassed. Here I had told her how different things were for a Spirit-filled Believer and how the power of the Holy Spirit works if one has faith.

Then, when at my lowest point of faith in our situation, I suddenly had the unction to try and start the motor. I got into the seat and hardly touched the key, and already it was running like a clock. Both of us sat there in utter amazement. Another lesson had to be learned: God will not necessarily do things our way. A Scripture then came to my mind: "Do not lean on your own understanding, in all your ways acknowledge Him" (Proverbs 3:5-6).

This was to be one of the hardest lessons to learn, one that even now, after decades of walking this path still presents a challenge that I struggle with.

The following day we had to buy a new battery. To our amazement, the old one was dead!

## Set Up Roadmarks...

We were now out of the mountains and were crossing the Wyoming Plains. Wanting to get an early start, I woke up that morning at about 4:00 a.m., walked into the kitchen area and saw my Bible open next to the sink. I was somewhat surprised, as I did not remember leaving it there. The flashlight lit up the open page and these verses jumped up at me as if they were on springs:

"Set up for yourself road marks, place for yourself guideposts, direct your heart to the highway, the way by which you went. Return, O virgin of Israel, return to these your cities. How long will you go here and there, O faithless daughter?" (Jeremiah 31: 21,22).

Tears started streaming down my face. I couldn't help but wail as if I had lost a loved one. I think my travel partner thought I had "gone off the deep end." How could I explain to her this longing in my heart for the Land of Israel?

There were no others that I knew of who behaved in this manner. But that morning it was really out of hand. For two hours I sobbed, wept and wiped the continual flow of tears from my eyes. Becky had to drive.

As we traveled east that morning the scene fit the Scriptures I had read: the big orange sun was coming up at the other end of the long, straight, desert highway.

We finally arrived in Wisconsin, where my sister and mother met us on the Interstate. Becky and I departed with a quick hug and I never heard from her again until twenty-five years later, when I received a letter from her.

## The Letter

Dear Ralph,

I have told my testimony for 25 years – perhaps an average of once a week for each of the past 25 years.

On Easter in 1976, I attended St. Timothy's Church. You were the only person who spoke to me and you told me that "Jesus loves you just the way you are." By August 26, 1976, I attended a court hearing for a car accident in which I had been drinking. I was an alcoholic, speed freak, and living with my boyfriend. The lawyer at the court hearing told me that I would be "crucified" if I lied on the stand.

I left the court hearing that day and I drove to St. Timothy's, completely suicidal. I did not find a pastor, but I found you. And you led me in the "sinner's" prayer, and in a prayer to receive the gifts of the Holy Spirit.

Within 24 hours, I quit drinking (both my father, aunt, and grandfather were lifetime alcoholics) and smoking dope, doing drugs, and you (1) helped me to find a room near the church to rent so that I could move out of my apartment with my boyfriend, and (2) you bought me a cassette tape player and the Bible (NT) on tape.

# Return to the Land

Within 2 months...it was apparent that I should return to Cleveland, Ohio and (miraculously) a man with 29 foot motor home paid me to drive his vehicle  back to his dealership in Ohio, by way of Wisconsin, where I dropped you off and stayed briefly with my sister.

I never saw or heard from you again.

You had told me that you were going to live in Israel – and be an evangelist. I, too, felt called to be an evangelist – after a "hand-laying, prophesying" impromptu event at your friends home on 3rd Street (or Avenue) in Monterey.

And that is what I became – and have never turned back.

I have had the opportunity to share my (our) story in 10 books, on network TV to 2.5 million people, on numerous Christian TV shows, at a Billy Graham Crusade in front of 40,000 people and at 30 events every year since 1984 (and with HS kids in  Cleveland for 10 years as a Youth For Christ staff worker!)

I married an evangelist who also was in YFC, we've been married 23 years and he is currently a pastoral counselor (very wise and mature, loving, and Christ-like). My son is 22, Jacob. A great kid still searching for his call in life, but (smile) I think it is evangelism, as well.

Ralph, I recently appeared on Focus on the Family with Dr. Dobson, a radio show that airs to 2.5 million people – daily – in America, and to millions more throughout the world. During the interview, he asked if I still knew you...and I said, I hadn't seen you since 1976 – but that you had told me you were going to Israel!

Your sister called my office and told my assistant that she was fairly certain that you were the "janitor" in my life! Because of you, thousands, perhaps 100's of 1000's have come to know Christ. And my favorite line has become, "if God is calling you today, let me be your janitor!"

I hope this letter encourages you.  I am having my 25th spiritual birthday on August 26th – I feel as if God wanted me to find you, both to validate the radical change in my life and His power to use both of us and fulfill the prophecy in our lives that we knew of 25 years ago – that for me is only now coming to pass!

FYI:  My maiden name was Becky Hunter.

Be encouraged,

Becky

## A Short, But Fruitful Stay

The two-week stay in Wisconsin, before flying back out to Monterey California, was filled with sharing new life with my sister and a small group of Believers whom The Lord had moved upon. I was also introduced to a retired Spirit-filled Methodist pastor, who had just started a prayer meeting in a federal correctional institute near my parents' home. He invited me to go with him. It was another one of those "only God could have done it" meetings.

# Return to the Land

Seven

# The Fleece

Returning to California was taking me in the opposite direction of the way I really wanted to go. I nonetheless settled back into the routines of life, but late in the winter of 1977 circumstances began to change. My job came to an end.

Should I look for another job, or not? That was my dilemma. Was this a sign that things were moving me on toward Israel? I had read how Gideon put fleeces out to see if God was in a certain matter. As I was learning not to trust my own feelings, I put out a fleece before the Lord. If He did not have work for me, which given the situation did not seem possible, I would consider that as a word to pack my bags and head east.

That morning I called a friend, who had told me that if I ever needed a job, there would always be one for me. My friend, Jim, who was Director of Special Education, answered the phone. With fear and trepidation I asked if there was an available position. To which he replied: "If you would have called me a half hour ago I would have had a place for you."

Joy shot through my soul like a lighting bolt. I couldn't wait to take the news to the prayer meeting that evening. At first I was a bit reluctant to share my thoughts, as I thought that some of the brethren would not confirm the timing of this move. However, everyone present was supportive and encouraging.

# Return to the Land

It only took me a couple of weeks to give away most of my belongings. Putting the rest of my possessions in the back of my truck, off I went, eastward, to Wisconsin.

Words from the Prophet Ezekiel carried me like the wings of an eagle: "I will take the children of Israel... and bring them into their own land; and I will make them one nation in the land, on the mountains of Israel..." (Ezekiel 37:21,22, NKJV).

## Saying Goodbye

Saying good bye to life in California, and to the many friends that bid me farewell, was not easy. Somehow we all knew that there was something final about this departure. I felt as if my roots had been dug up, and that I was suspended in mid air.

However, as my little blue truck and I streamed down that same highway that I had traveled nine months before in the motor home, thoughts of that early morning Scripture began to ring through my mind: "Direct your heart to the highway, the way by which you went. Return, O virgin of Israel return to these your cities."

The trip to Wisconsin was uneventful, except for a little side excursion in Iowa, to visit my Alma Mater. That brief visit made me realize that my life before being born from above, born of the Spirit, was akin to a dream in the night.

## Repentance Road

Arriving back at my parents' home was like stepping into a time machine which took me to the days when I had still lived there. Fifteen years had passed, but here I was, back in my old room, working with my father on the farm in the cucumber sorting station that he had taken over from his father!

The Lord was giving me many opportunities to share the new Spirit-filled life with old friends and family.

Amazingly, the community began to grow rapidly as His grace drew many into the "life in the Spirit."

In a town of about 150 people this move did not escape the notice of the die-hard traditional Lutherans. What was happening all around bothered the town folk and the minister. The latter had actually preached a few sermons on the subject of speaking in tongues, telling everyone why he felt it should not be done. He also spoke against the other spiritual gifts, and against their relevance for today. He even found it necessary to pay me a visit!

The Spirit was also moving in the prison ministry, so much so that I was invited to share at other prisons. The excitement of seeing a community of Believers being raised up in my hometown had actually taken my mind somewhat off Israel.

During the summer the elderly Methodist pastor asked me if I wanted to drive down to Kansas City for a Holy Spirit conference, which I did. I do not remember much about that conference, except for one meeting that took place between Jewish and Gentile Believers.

## Reconciliation

This was the first time I had witnessed reconciliation through repentance and the washing of feet between these two estranged groups of people. Everyone in the room was moved. They were crying, laughing and hugging each other.

I knew something powerful was happening, but could not put my finger on what it was. It somehow felt that this was a reunion of long lost family members, although I had not quite grasped what it all meant.

Working with my father again and being around my mother, who both treated me as if I were still seventeen, presented a challenge. To my surprise, many attitudes that I had toward them as a rebellious teenager surfaced again. My parents hadn't changed, and neither had I.

# Return to the Land

I did not realize until years later, God's wisdom in bringing me back home. There were still bitterness, resentment and rebellious sarcasm in me, and the Lord was after it.

One night, as I was going out the door, my mother asked me where I was going and when would I return.

I was stunned at my irritated and very emotional response, which does not bear repeating. She was shocked and so was I.

"Where did that come from?" I asked myself. Much of the refuse of my life-long attitude was being uncovered. Change had to take place in me before the Heavenly Father would release me to go to the Land of Israel.

That little portion of Scripture, "Return by the way in which you went," was not referring only to a physical high-way—those dangling exposed roots were important to the Husbandman. If He were going to transplant a healthier shoot, repentance had to first spring forth in me.

As my rebellious attitudes were being exposed, the Spirit was bringing to my remembrance those Scriptures in Romans that had been so meaningful five years previously: "They are violent, proud, boasters, inventors of evil things, disobedient to parents, undiscerning, untrustworthy, unloving, unforgiving, unmerciful."

The Holy Spirit was not waiting for me to go to some church service to repent, it was in the heat of the moment that He was ready to administer forgiveness, deliverance and healing to my soul. I also realized that the verse which says, "With weeping they shall come and by supplication I will lead them," had to do with a deep repentance from the sins of youth. Repentance is one of the tools for removing the debris and the stones from this "highway of return."

## On My Way

The cucumber-growing season was coming to an end,

but my involvement with the local believing community was growing. However, one morning I read Ezekiel chapters two and three, and again my attention was drawn to the Land and its people.

My dad paid me for the work I had done that summer, and with that money I bought a stand-by plane ticket for a six-week trip to Israel.

## On the Faith Road Again

The day had finally arrived, and I was ready to leave. Excitement aptly describes my feelings then, although not knowing anyone in the Land, I was a little nervous about going alone.

My only lead for a possible contact were the names of an American couple living on a Christian kibbutz.

When I arrived in Chicago, after a four hour bus ride and a check-in process at the airport, the stewardess informed me that I would be unable to take the flight, as it had been over booked. I could not believe my ears. I was just about to walk away, when for some reason I decided to sit down on a bench in the waiting area, where I had a little chat with the Lord. It went something like this: "If this is as far as I get to go to Israel, at least it was a start. But was my timing off?" I asked.

As I was sitting there, chin in hands, I heard my name being called. The lady at the desk beckoned to me with her finger. I approached the desk with what must have been a forlorn expression. "There is one seat left on this flight, so hurry down the ramp and a stewardess will direct you," she said.

I flew down the ramp, my feet hardly, if at all, touching the rubber mat. When I arrived, a beautiful little brunette led me to a window seat in first class. Tears welled up in my eyes as she put a tablecloth on the table in front of me with a wine glass and a small bottle of wine. All I would have needed was just a piece of bread, and I would have felt as Abraham must have done when approached by Melchizedec.

It was a warm clear "Indian summer" day as the plane lifted off the runway. The trees were still in their Fall colors, although many had already lost their leaves by then. Soon we were high above the blue water of Lake Michigan, heading east toward New York. I tilted back my seat, enjoying the first class treatment and just worshiped in what seemed to be the only appropriate form: "spirit and truth."

Joy and peace engulfed my soul as I noticed outside the window a few small fluffy white clouds scattered below. They looked like little sheep grazing in a pasture of blue. As I was musing over the little flock below, it grew and soon formed endless rows of "puffs," as far as my eye could see. I watched this army march toward the east, until it formed a huge thunderhead, which had taken a kind of prophetic meaning or significance. It seemed God was showing me a picture of what He was going to do with the lost sheep of the House of Israel. He was gathering them one by one into flocks, which would take the form of a marching army, to ultimately become an expression of His power, light and sustenance to the earth below, as expressed in Psalm 104:3: "He makes the clouds His [military] chariot."

Those clouds also reminded me of a word He had dropped into my mind when our High Adventure tour was traveling down the Arava (desert) road toward Massada (on my first visit). The dry desert scenery contrasted with what we seemed to represent as a group of Believers. Although we were nothing more than a mist that appears but for a moment, yet it was as though by His presence in us we were watering a seed that would soon sprout and break forth.

Thrilled by the thought, I had shared it with others in the group, and we all sensed the significance of being in the Land at that time.

# Eight

# The Holy Land?

Arriving in the Land as a lone gullible greenhorn American tourist left me vulnerable to veteran vultures. They were waiting there for "a piece of meat" like me, or for whomever else they could devour, alive or dead.

No doubt that many are familiar with this type of bird. Because of them, I had to learn some lessons about the Lord being my Shepherd, about experiencing divine appointments, and entertaining angels unaware.

Soon these things seemed almost routine, as though they were part of ordinary life.

As I walked out of the terminal suitcase in hand, with "wondering-what-to-do" written all over my face, a kindly taxi driver was willing to help me, for a goodly sum of dollars, of course. But my God had another plan. At that moment a lovely couple walked up to me and suggested we share a taxi, since the three of us were heading for Tel Aviv. When we arrived at our destination, they paid for the ride, and the driver took me to a very nice and inexpensive hotel where I settled in for the night with a very thankful heart.

I woke up quite early the next morning and decided to go outside and get my bearings, or at least try to. To my surprise I was only one block away from the beach, so in the cool morning air I walked the beautiful beach giving thanks to a wonderful Heavenly Father.

After eating the usual Israeli hotel breakfast of hard-boiled eggs, bread, cheeses, vegetables, and raw fish (which I didn't even attempt), I sat in my room, wondering what I should do.  I decided to call the Christian Kibbutz, which was up North, and see if I could come and visit the place at some point during my stay.  Off I went down the hall, to use the public phone.  The phone machine would not take any of the Israeli coins that I tried to put into its strange little slot in the front.  Just at that moment a man walked out of his room, and asked me in English if I needed help. He explained to me about the phone tokens that needed to be purchased and gave me one to use. Later I ran into this man again. He seemed quite friendly and suggested we go out on the town together.  This gentleman was an Israeli Arab from Nazareth who worked for the government, and was in town on business. Together we went to what turned out to be a nightclub where my eyes were open to triple or quadruple x-rated stage shows.

## Bursting My Bubble

I saw the "Holy Land" from a different angle.  Maybe the Lord had in mind to burst my "holy people" bubble and teach me something new.

The following day, after beholding the unexpected the night before, I walked around gazing into shop windows, listening to the sights and sounds of a very busy city.  I was a little familiar with the Hebrew language, as I had picked up a few words and simple phrases from a tape that I had purchased on my first trip. It felt so good to be in the Land. Home sweet home!  The sights, sounds and smells were all foreign but everything inside of me kept burning with excitement at every step. Quite by chance I ran into a marketplace (called a "shook") and mingled with the rest of the shoppers.

They were packed shoulder to shoulder; some holding shopping bags, others pulling little pull carts. As I pushed my way through the crowd, which seemed to be the custom, I could hear on both sides young and old men shouting out the prices of their merchandise, which was stacked up in little red, orange, yellow and green hills. The merchants would fling a couple of plastic bags in front of the potential buyer, who would then throw into those bags the quantity of fruit or vegetables desired, handing them over to the vendor, who would weigh it on old lead scales. Sometimes it took several extra pieces, or a few less, to make up the desired weight. Currency would be exchanged and the person would walk away feeling that they had just gotten the best deal in town. As for me, I would not have trusted a single one of those characters. They reminded me of the men who worked the fairs and circuses in the States.

After spending an amusing day on the streets of Tel Aviv, I again ran into the Arab gentleman from Nazareth, this time in the lobby of the hotel. He approached me and said that he had set up a date for me for that evening, and that all of us would go out for a good time at a theater and then dancing. This was quite a surprise, since he had not informed me of these plans, nor did he even bother to ask me if I wanted to go.

I had wondered, do I have a choice in this matter? Is this the way things are done on this side of the world? Being a polite American Christian I thanked him for looking out after me and agreed to be ready at a certain time.

I waited outside as he brought his car to the front of the hotel. We drove off to pick up a young lady, who was a secretary in the office that he worked in. The theater show was a little risqué, but nothing like the night before! The disco was a bit out of my league, but I tried to have fun anyway. My date turned out to be a very nice young lady, a little plump but quite attractive and friendly, although I had the impression that she was somewhat disappointed by her date.

## Up to Jerusalem

The following morning I took leave of Tel-Aviv and went up to Jerusalem.

Just before leaving, my friend from Nazareth invited me to come and stay at his home. I wrote down his name and telephone number and agreed that at some point in my stay I would come to Nazareth and look him up.

After the usual breakfast, I checked out of the hotel, suitcase in hand, but not after first inquiring for the bus to the Central Bus Station. Armed with that information, I strode to the bus stop that displayed the appropriate number, but soon after it occurred to me that I needed a ticket. With that thought I approached a little booth next to the bus stop, asking the man sitting inside for a ticket. He pushed a ticket in my direction, took the amount from the bill that I gave him, and continued reading his newspaper. As I walked back to the bus, I thought to myself that the ticket was a little expensive, but before I had a chance to go back and check, the bus drove up.

Half walking and half being carried on the shoulders of the crowd pushing their way to the bus, I managed to keep my balance and found myself inside. At one point my suitcase and arm ended up behind two other people, but eventually I managed to establish my place within the mob. I soon noticed that the other passengers were making their way to a little window, where a man seemed to be selling tickets. When my turn came, if it could even be termed that, I proudly displayed my pass for the ride. When the ticket seller took it from my hand, he turned it over and looked up at me with a smile. I noticed that others were also laughing and smiling.

Eventually he announced in broken English and in a voice that to me seemed a little too loud, that this was not a bus ticket but a lottery ticket and that I needed to purchase from him the regular bus pass.

In my embarrassment I told him to keep the lottery ticket. Surprised, he excitedly said something about the prospect of winning, and told me that he had eight children, adding that maybe this was his lucky day. As I turned around, and with all eyes fixed on me, I tried to quietly hide in the corner. Suddenly two men who spoke English asked me where I was headed.

To my surprise, after I had told them what my destination was, they responded: "We are also on our way to Jerusalem, why don't you just tag along."

"Tag" seemed the appropriate word in my condition, although I did feel a sense of relief and that God had just tucked me under the wings of a couple of angels. As the bus flew down the narrow streets, I was now feeling much more comfortable.

Fortunately we were well packed inside the bus, or we would have been thrown from side to side. I had full admiration for the skills of the driver, as at times there seemed to be only a hair's breadth between the bus and other vehicles.

## A Faith-Filled Sherut Ride

We finally arrived at the bus station, but instead of taking a bus to Jerusalem the guys informed me of another form of transpiration called *"sherut."*

A sherut taxi was an extra large vehicle, which accommodated about ten passengers. They said that if it filled up, everyone would split the cost and that it was about the same price as the bus. It did not take long to fill the taxi.

After the driver tied down the luggage on the top rack, we were off... And what a ride we were in for!

At that time the Jerusalem-Tel Aviv road was not the four-lane highway that it is today. Instead it was only two lanes, and it was crooked, but this did not seem to deter the driver from speeding.

# Return to the Land

I was sitting in the middle behind the front seat and could hardly believe what I was experiencing! The driver was passing cars on blind curves. I don't think I took a breath all the way from Tel Aviv to Jerusalem.

When I looked at the other passengers, they were as calm as could be. I wasn't sure which Jerusalem I would be ending up in: Earthly or Heavenly. The driver surely drew me closer to God than any preacher I had ever known.

# Nine

# A Room at the Inn

After arriving in (the earthly) Jerusalem safe and not so sound, I was given directions on how to get to the YMCA via a city bus. No more taxis for me!

Entering the castle-like building, the reception desk was just ahead of me, so without hesitation I inquired about a room. When the clerk announced that none were available, a slight sinking feeling crept into my stomach. But as I was about to leave, a man who was standing behind the clerk turned around and said something to the latter in a language that was not Hebrew. I thought perhaps it was Arabic. Turning to me and addressing me as "Sir," the clerk said that there was only one very small room that they did not usually use, but because this was a feast day they would make an exception. It would be mine, if I so wished.

It was a relief to have this little room and to just rest in a mode of thankfulness. As I lay on the little cot, I randomly opened my Bible and read these words: "It is good to give thanks to The Lord and to sing praises to Thy name, O most High; To declare Thy loving kindness in the morning and Thy faithfulness by night."

My eyes closed and I fell asleep like a little lamb in the arms of his loving shepherd. I slept from about four o'clock in the afternoon to 2:30 in the morning. When I awoke, I was not sure where I was for a second. Light from a street lamp barely allowed me to see the only light switch in the room. I gingerly made my way down the hall to the washroom, which turned out to be a little stall. Yes, it certainly was little!

The door opened in as far as the commode, so I had to squeeze between the wall and the door in order to close it. The reverse was true in getting out. A person of different dimensions would have had to give up any plans to use this facility. Being no engineer or architect, it still seemed to me that they should have had the door open to the outside. There was no lock on the door, which was understandable, as it would have been impossible to open it anyway while in use.

I spent most of the night, or early morning hours, writing letters home, reading Scriptures and daydreaming until it was time for breakfast. No surprises awaited me there. The same menu that was served in the hotel in Tel Aviv was now laid out in the Jerusalem YMCA.

For a couple of days I wandered around the city, getting acquainted with the old and new sections. I ran into a few spots that I recognized from my first trip over. I also met tourists who informed me of a Holy Spirit Conference that was taking place at the Diplomat Hotel.

## Project Kibbutz

While attending some of the conference meetings, I met Jim and Ginger from Idabel, Oklahoma. We became friends and exchanged telephone numbers and addresses. On one of those conference days I also met a couple of young volunteers from a nearby kibbutz.

They told me about a discipleship training program that they were on called Project Kibbutz. It called for a one year commitment to work and study with a group of ten to fifteen Christians on a kibbutz, which is a type of cooperate community unique to Israel. I thought that would be a wonderful way to experience the Land.

A week or so later, when attending a Shabbat service

at Jerusalem's Baptist Congregation, I met the director of the volunteer program for Project Kibbutz. We seemed to hit it off and he invited me to go with him to visit a couple of the kibbutzim (plural for "kibbutz") which were connected to the Project. They were located in the vicinity of Jerusalem.

One night, on the way back from a visit to one of those kibbutzim, I had a strong feeling that God was going to open the doors to some kibbutzim in northern Israel. When I mentioned it to Art he looked at me, quite surprised, as if I had just gotten in on a secret, but he responded nonchalantly, "If God wants that to happen He will have to make it possible."

## Ephraim?

During the tour that I was on the year before, we stopped at a Christian kibbutz in the Western Galilee. Since I already had the name of the American couple living there, I called them and made arrangements to visit. A day or so before my departure from Jerusalem, I was invited to a prayer meeting at an apartment in town where I met a Jewish Believer who had been thrown out of an absorption center for new immigrants—for allegedly sharing with someone that she was a Believer in Jesus. She told me that she was in hiding, as the Ministry (that is the government office or department) for Interior Affairs was threatening to have her deported. She also said that she was going back up to her hiding place in Nahariya, and that it was not too far from the Christian kibbutz I wanted to visit. We agreed to travel together the following day, which was a Friday. While on our way, Esther suggested we stop by and visit one of the few Messianic congregations in the Land and have a Kabbalat Shabbat meal (a festive meal with prayers and song to welcome the Sabbath) with some of the local Believers.

# Return to the Land

The meeting place turned out to be a spacious villa in a resort town along the coast. By the time we arrived, other Believers, who came from different places in the country to attend the fellowship, were already there.

As I walked into the living room, I noticed a woman sitting on the sofa. When I introduced myself with the typical American greeting "Hi, my name is Ralph," she responded in a way that overwhelmed me.

Repeating my name in a very strong and exaggerated New York accent, "Rrraa-llfff!" She then added: "Your name should not be Ralph, it should be Ephraim."

I couldn't imagine what had induced her to say what she did, but since I was not about to change my name her comment was left to hang in midair.

## Kabbalat Shabbat

The evening meal was very festive with lots of food, drink, stories and songs; some in Hebrew, and some in English. Since public transportation stops when the Shabbat comes in on Friday afternoon, I was wondering if everyone would be staying for the evening and for the next day (as none of those present appeared to have arrived by car).

Sure enough, when the time came, everyone just grabbed a thin foam mattress and simply found a place to sleep on the floor. I chose the open balcony on the roof.

I didn't get much sleep that night. I kept gazing up at the night sky, watching the same stars and planets that Abraham was given to count so many thousands of years ago. I kept feeling deep inside myself that somehow I was one of those little stars, an offspring that God had promised to that Patriarch as he stood there looking up at the same universe.

The early morning sunrise was just glorious, to say the least. Worship of the Creator was not too difficult in such a beautiful setting.

After a breakfast of cereal and *challa* (Shabbat loaf)
we all sat around and fellowshipped until it was time for
the meeting. The service was in Hebrew with English
translation, although most of us, if not all, were English
speakers. We stayed again through Saturday night and
left the next morning for Nahariya.

## On to the Kibbutz

The bus was packed to the utmost, so I gave up my
seat to an elderly lady. After about two hours of clinging
to the standing rod, in that hot, stuffy, smoke-filled
environment, I was beginning to wonder if I hadn't
landed in hell.

At one point I happened to look down at the elderly
lady and saw numbers tattooed on her arm. I remembered my tour through the Holocaust Memorial, and had
wondered what was the survival story of the lady that I
had given my seat to. She sat there very serenely, as if it
was just a joy to be alive in spite of the discomfort.

We arrived at the Nahariya bus station none too soon.
Bidding everyone a short good bye, my clandestine travel
partner directed me to my bus. Within a half an hour I
was dropped off at a bus stop, from which point I had to
walk about three kilometers (more than one mile) to the
kibbutz itself. It was a hot and humid day, reminding me
of the good old summer months in Wisconsin.

The kibbutz office was a welcoming sight, as the
receptionist poured me a glass of cold water. She and her
husband were the ones that I was to stay with while
there. Lev was still out in the avocado orchard,
handpicking the ones that were ready for harvest. I
joined him there during my few days visit.

Having grown up on a farm, this life seemed the most
natural for me. Before leaving I asked the kibbutz
management if I could apply for membership. The
request was denied, as the church organization (which

# Return to the Land

was Scandinavian, if I recall correctly) already had their quota of Americans (consisting of my hosts) and I had a feeling they were two too many, as far as the Europeans were concerned.

## Ten

# A Different Culture

Before leaving on my travels to the Christian kibbutz, I was told about two believing brothers (of the flesh and blood species) who resided in Rosh Pina ("Head of the Cornerstone") in the Upper Galilee. As I studied the map, I noticed that Nazareth was right on the way to that village. I remembered the standing invitation to visit my Arab friend, and decided to call him.

Ibrahim sounded delighted at the prospect of my visit and asked me to stay for a couple of days. I felt obliged to accept.

Again using Israel's wonderful transportation system, I arrived in downtown Nazareth in the late morning. The Arab flavor of the town was very apparent. I inquired with one of the merchants about my friend's family, and he immediately knew who I meant and directed me to the right home.

Ibrahim's home was a very big, relatively new and beautiful villa. When I met my host's eleven children, I realized why he needed such a big house.

The kitchen area had a gas counter stove, a refrigerator and a couple of cabinets. A heavy wooden table, with very high-back ornate chairs made of equally heavy wood, took up the dinning area. Some pictures decorated the living room walls and the floor was covered with a large Oriental rug, but otherwise I do not recall seeing too many pieces of furniture in that room.

I was escorted to my bedroom, which had a wooden bed of the same style as the dinning room table. I left my suitcase there.

After being served a cup of very sweet tea, my host took me on a quick tour of the town. When we completed the rounds, Ibrahim inquired if I had ever been to a Bedouin camp. Having found out that I hadn't, he asked me for ten dollars so that he could buy a gift for his Bedouin friend whom we were about to visit. I gave him the money, but there was no change for whatever it was that he purchased.

## Tea Time

The Bedouin campsite was situated out of town. From this point onward there was no more English; for the rest of the time I was to be entertained in Arabic. I was introduced to two Bedouin men who spoke to me as if I had understood every word.

The four of us sat cross-legged on rugs around an open fire with coals, which held three brass teapots. I had never seen anything like this before, and was fascinated as our host poured hot water from the large pot to the medium one, which contained the tea. Then, after a while, he filled the smallest of the three kettles, which may have had some herbs in it. He later poured the content into very small glasses, not much bigger than whiskey tumblers, and served them on a tray.

The glass was as hot as the tea inside, and was almost impossible to pick off the tray. I had a choice of either placing it immediately down on the rug, or requiring first aid. My hosts all smiled and raised their glasses as a welcoming gesture toward me.

All of a sudden the tent began to shake violently. Dust started falling from its ceiling. I almost jumped out of my skin, but it did not seem to bother the others. As I looked out of the opening of the tent, thinking of making a quick escape, my eye caught a large billy goat rubbing its horns against one of the tent ropes. Somewhat relieved, I settled back down to my glass of tea that I was now able to pick up by the rim.

To my dismay, I noticed particles, which had descended from the tent's ceiling, floating on top of my drink. The men watching me were quite amused at their "gringo" guest.

After tea time I was taken to a large mound of dirt that had smoke coming out of small portholes on its sides. Even though the sight was strange, the smell was familiar. I was informed that my Bedouin host had a charcoal business. The process of making the charcoal was not so different from the way my father made it in his kilns in Wisconsin, where I had worked most summers as a youth.

## The Rimon

After returning to my host's home he left me to rest, as he himself prepared for, and participated in the Muslim evening prayers. Upon his return we enjoyed a very wonderful meal, which was topped by a very interesting looking fruit for dessert that can only be described as a "crowned apple."

*"Rimon"* in Hebrew and "pomegranate" in English was the answer I was given to my question regarding this strange fruit.

A surprise awaited me as I started to slowly cut into it with my knife. It was as if I had just cut into a living creature, as the juice that flowed out was blood-like. Finally I saw all the little succulent seeds, and slowly began to chew them, sucking their juice while taking care not to bite too hard on the seed and not to stain my clothing with a spurt of the crimson liquid.

Although the process was tedious, yet there was something very strangely prophetic about that fruit.

# Return to the Land

Little did I know that the Lord had a special "Rimona" planned for me.

The bed in the guest bedroom was very comfortable, and I fell asleep quite readily after a long day.

Very quickly I came to understand why everyone retired early. At about 4:00 a.m. I was jolted out of my sleep by the sounds of a minaret just outside my window. It was a foreboding sound, followed by the prayers that resounded out of that tower.

I heard my host rise and begin his day with the first of the five installments of worship the Muslims engage in during the course of a 24-hour period. Not able to sleep anymore, I quietly lay in bed until about 6:00 a.m., when I heard my name being called for breakfast.

Later, I joined my host on a business engagement he had in the West Bank town of Jenin. We went to a factory located there that made winter coats for the Israeli Army. When back in Nazareth, in mid-afternoon, Ibrahim asked me if I wanted barbequed meat. Without waiting for a response, he requested 20 dollars for the purchase of a chop of lamb. Just as before, the amount I gave him seemed to cover the cost to the last penny. I then had another one of those cultural surprises.

Although the fire for the barbeque was started outdoors, when the coals were ready Ibrahim brought them, along with the grill, to the kitchen setting the whole thing on the floor and proceeded to cook the meat right there and then. We sat on the floor waiting for the meat to cook, which was a good idea as everything above us filled with smoke. I did not have it in me to ask him why this was being performed in the kitchen.

After a very tasty meal he asked me a number of leading questions, ultimately arriving at what was on his mind. Ibrahim wanted two of his oldest children to go with me to the States, where I was to help them get into a university in Wisconsin. Since it seemed that, under the circumstances, etiquette did not permit a negative response, I left the issue high up in the air...

## Rosh Pina

Leaving Nazareth for Rosh Pina, the following day, I was, in some way, very relieved. I had had enough of the Islamic culture. It was a welcome reprieve to be again with other Believers. Reuven and Benjamin seemed to be well known in this little town, in view of the fact that their activities as Jewish Believers in the Messiah were about as welcome as a bear in a beehive. Their home was vandalized and there was an attempt to set it on fire, as some of local anti-missionary groups tried to encourage them to leave the area. As a matter of fact, they were expecting more problems the very day I arrived.

Rosh Pina is an old Jewish town, with narrow cobblestone roads and quaint little houses. It is set on the side of a mountain on top of which sits the famous town of *Tzfat*, from where one can see out across the open fields all the way down into the Hula Valley and on over to the Golan Heights.

Being with the brothers was refreshing. It was a time of being spiritually built up. We shared testimonies, only to find out that our fathers may have been somehow connected in the fur trade business. At the brothers' home I met a number of Believers who stopped by to fellowship. One of them was a big burly man, whom I thought might have looked like Peter, Yeshua's disciple. His family had just been voted off a kibbutz because of their beliefs and obvious evangelistic tendencies.

## The Black Mountain

My days in Israel were winding down much too fast, and I had to bid good-bye to my glorious Galilee experience. I really did not want to leave, but felt that it still was not the time to settle there. As I reflected on the experiences and the meetings I had with Believers from across the entire Land, I asked the Lord why this small community was so spread out and so diversified.

He gave me the answer in a dream. I saw a map of the State of Israel and over it was what looked like a spider web. I sensed that the web was His love, and that the Believers were the connecting links in the web. As I contemplated the dream, I thought of the effectiveness of the web as a trap while Yeshua spins His love throughout the country by means of those who believe in Him, in contrast to a web that is made up into one ball (of religious conformity).

During that time I had another interesting dream. I saw a big black mountain next to an ocean. Suddenly a huge wave came up out of the sea and crashed up against this mountain with a force that broke it up into black and dark gray boulders. Later, another wave appeared. This time, it had in it faces of people from the days of the Reformation. When this wave made its way back off the big black boulders, it had broken them up into smaller rocks and large stones. The next wave again had many faces of people like Billy Graham, Oral Roberts, Derek Prince and others.

Like the previous wave, it too went up upon the shore of rocks and stones, and when it receded, the shore was full of multicolored pebbles, and collectively they made a beautiful sight.

This wave also receded back into the ocean, with another one appearing right behind it. This one was a wave that looked like seeds. It made its way up on the beach of pebbles, and as it disappeared back into the sea it left the beach with white glistening sand. The final wave was one of fire. It went up over the sand, but did not withdraw. Rather, it was absorbed by the white sands, turning the entire area into glass and obliterating the shoreline which was no longer distinct from the ocean, as it too had turned into glass.

At the time I was not sure of the dream's

interpretation, however, reflecting on the meaning of this dream at a later stage, it seemed that the large black mountain was the House of Jacob, with the first wave being the apostolic wave of the first outpouring of the Holy Spirit after the Messiah took up His position in the heavens.

The second wave signified the moving of the Holy Spirit in what history calls the Reformation. The third wave represented the nineteenth and twentieth centuries' world evangelism, and Pentecostal and Charismatic movements. The wave of seed started to rise during the twentieth century, as there is always a time overlap in the course of these changes. And almost as naturally as one wave resists the next, so it is with these movements.

This fourth wave, which we seem to be in at this time, is the working of the Holy Spirit in restoring the identity of the seed of Abraham, Isaac and Jacob. This restoration will lead to the final wave of fire when "the house of Jacob will be a fire and the house of Joseph a flame" (Obadiah 1:18, NKJV).

# Return to the Land

# Eleven

# Released

As I was checking in my suitcase for the flight back to the States, I was torn inside again with the thought of leaving home. My thoughts were very far from the young lady who was trying to extract answers out of me. I think she somehow felt my sadness and was being compassionate. As she closed my suitcase, and marked it with a little yellow tag, the comforting thoughts of the Spirit reminded me of the words that the Lord gave me after my tour, a year and half before: "Be strong and of good courage."

Once on the jet, I relaxed and submitted to His will. Peace descended upon my soul, as I pulled my Bible out from the carry-on bag. My fingers were almost like metal to a magnet, as they opened the pages to Ezekiel. "But you, O mountains of Israel, you shall shoot forth your branches and yield your fruit to My people Israel, for they are about to come...I will multiply men upon you, all the house of Israel, all of it... Yes, I will cause men to walk on you, My people Israel; they shall take possession of you, and you shall be their inheritance" (Ezekiel 36:8,10,12).

## Chilly Wisconsin

Arriving back in Wisconsin in November was a chilling contrast to the warm Mediterranean climate. The sudden change quickly brought me back to reality.

Though the climate was cold, my family and the community of Believers greeted me very warmly. Their love helped me settle back into a routine of assisting my sister with her home school, and my dad with the odd jobs he had for me. But what was most rewarding were the times spent in the prison, teaching the prisoners about their new life in the Spirit. I had forgotten how cold Wisconsin could be in January, so I made arrangements to go back to California to thaw out and visit my friends.

It was wonderful to see and reminisce with brothers and sisters in the faith. There was still a handful that held the vision for Israel, but most of those who had been on the original tour slipped back into their American life style and forgot all about their zeal for the Land.

Nevertheless, one young and enthusiastic couple, Sal and Linda, were on their way to live in the Land for as long as the door would be kept open. Sal was a very talented musician and handyman and Linda was a hair stylist. They thought that perhaps they would be able to find employment and settle in Israel.

Another brother who had not lost his fiery and prophetic zeal was putting the final touches on his book called "The Last Trumpet." Norman was the one who had taken us all on the High Adventure tour.

I read Norman's manuscript while I stayed with him for a few days. His prophetic and discerning eye was evident. He spun a story that contained some personal life data and descriptions of his experiences in the church system. He pointed out very graphically how most of the divisions in the Body of Believers was the result of the "mind set of the Tree of Knowledge of Good and Evil."

He explained how that thought process would inevitably lead to a humanistic approach to the gospel and to a one world religious system. That religious order would then join up with the world's political, oil and economic cartels to wage war against Jerusalem and

Israel. He prophesied that the Palestinians would rise up, with a UN backing, to establish a Palestinian state in the West Bank and Gaza. This would be accomplished by terrorist activity of the kind never seen before. Young men and children would strap bombs to their bodies and blow themselves up in public places. This kind of terror would lead many in the secular State of Israel to leave, but at the same time the Jewish Zionist zealots would stand and fight. He made mention of "a faith people" that would appear at that time, and join the Jews in defending the Land and Jerusalem for the soon coming Messiah.

Time would prove how accurate his predictions were, but because he strongly opposed the pre-tribulation rapture, his book never made it into the world of mesmerized Christianity.

## Idabel

I left California after a wonderful two week stay, and headed for some more warm country. This time it was to Idabel, a small country town in Okalahoma, to visit Jim and Ginger, whom I had met five months before in Jerusalem. After a flight to Dallas and a long bus ride to Idabel, I met Jim at the bus station.

My stay with Jim and Ginger was filled with divine appointments and a lot of conversation.

One such meeting was with a neighbor's wife who came for spiritual counsel. I do not remember what I said to her, but apparently it had a healing effect. She and her husband had broken up and the loss she suffered had been quite devastating. Two years later, while already living in Israel, I received a "thank you" letter from her, with a tiny woman's engagement ring tucked inside another very small envelope. The postscript went something like: "Please do not send this back to me, I know you are supposed to have it."

# Return to the Land

Feeling very indifferent toward the gift, I put it back into its envelope and stuffed it somewhere in the pages of my Bible.

Jim had arranged for me to share at a prayer meeting in a nearby prison. But a couple of days before the prison visit, we went to a small country Baptist church that was having a "revival," where I had been asked to share. My small portion of the revival meeting was to sing a song, the lyrics to which I had partially adapted from a pop tune called "Burning Bridges." To these lyrics I added some words from the old hymn, "The Old Rugged Cross." For me, this old hymn, which I had sung in church many times, expressed the message of salvation for a world of lost sinners. The verses and chorus went like this:

> All the rugged crosses that have fallen after me,
> All the lonely feelings and the burning memories,
> All His love I left behind each time I closed the door,
> Rugged crosses lost forever more.
> Jesus tried to warn me, but I held my head up high,
> All the time He warned me but I only passed Him by,
> Jesus tried to tell me, but I guess I didn't care,
> Turned my back and left Him standing there.
> Jesus tried to help me find the way, long ago;
> When I finally saw it, I didn't want to go.
> He died upon that cross for me, but I didn't really care
> Turned my back and left Him hanging there.
> Years have passed and I keep thinking "what a fool I've been."
> I look into the past and think of Him back then
> I know I've lost everything I thought I could win.
> I guess I should have listened to Him then.

Many people seemed to be touched by the song, as tears weld up in their eyes. The pastor made an altar call afterwards and quite a few came forward to rededicate their lives to their living Messiah.

The occasion was quite memorable, but nothing like

that which took place after the meeting! Instead of leaving the building by the front door and going out for fellowship, I slipped through the back door.

As I opened it, only to be flooded by the bright noon sunlight, an almost audible voice said to me, *"Go to Israel now!"*

My immediate response was to protest. "Now?! But the doors are opening to the prison ministry!"

Again I heard "NOW!!"

Jim suddenly appeared around the corner, and taking one look at me he said: "Are you all right?"

I think my face appeared rather white and I was quite shaken. All that I could get out of my mouth was: "Could you take me to the bus? I have to go to Israel now!"

Jim did not ask me any questions, as he instinctively knew that this was of the Lord.

Later that afternoon I started my two-day journey back up to Wisconsin on a Greyhound bus.

## Everyone Knew

Having had this blessing from above to go back to the Land was exciting, and as a result, during the entire tiring trip back to Wisconsin my mind was occupied with extrapolating possible scenarios for the future.

It was a relief to arrive at my parents' home and to get some sleep in a nice warm bed, after those two days of sitting on buses and spending time in not too pleasant bus depots.

I couldn't wait to shout out to all I met that I was going back to Israel. But for some reason I didn't have to. Everyone already seemed to know that it was time. Even my dad, who at one point was quite upset at the thought of me leaving and going to live in Israel, warmed up to the idea.

Nevertheless, one day, as he and I were eating lunch together, he looked at me from across the kitchen table in a very businesslike manner and in much the same tone said: "Well Ralph, I'm gonna be retiring soon and I would like for you to take over some of the businesses."

Knowing that this was no small matter to him, and being taken by surprise by this statement, his words found me lost for a reply.

Almost instantly a paraphrase of a Scripture popped out of my memory banks and into my conscious thoughts: "If you leave father and mother, sisters and brothers, houses and farms, for the sake of the gospel of the kingdom, I will add to you fathers and mothers, sisters and brothers, houses and farms" (reference Mark 10:29).

Conversing with my dad was not necessarily natural to me. However, for some reason in that moment, as our eyes met, it seemed as though eternity stopped and father and son united in one of those rare moments. The answer flowed out of my mouth with unexpected ease: "Well Dad, you know that I've given my life to Jesus and I feel I need to go to Israel."

Rather than a display of anger, tears began to form in his eyes; simultaneously we both rose from our positions, almost as though we were connected physically.

We met under the kitchen light, and with tears streaming down our cheeks we embraced. Without any exchange of words, I knew I had been released from that obligation. But more than that, I felt I had my father's blessing to go out and share the good news.

## Blessed and Released

A change took place on that special dark and foggy February day. There was lightness in my heart that I had not had before. I was a man who had been given his father's blessing, and was released to go with my God.

Later that day I started making arrangements for my travel to Israel. The following morning I drove to the travel agent's office, not really expecting a cheap ticket, nor a date that would be as soon as I would have liked. But by this time I was starting to get used to divine interventions, so I was quite relaxed as I walked into the office, wondering what was in store for me.

While waiting for my turn, however, I had time to think, a fact that resulted in some fear and anxiety.

By the time the agent was free to receive me, I had failed the test of waiting upon the Lord and being at rest.

My heart was racing as she shuffled a few papers. She then looked up at me and said, "Well Mr. Frank, I'm sorry. I couldn't find anything that would give you some kind of a financial break, but I noticed a TWA special for an open ticket up to a year."

This deal surprised both of us, as it was quite unusual for airlines to do this, especially in their flights to Israel. Without hesitation I inquired about the dates. "February 22nd" was the answer. The price was beyond the amount that I had on hand, but the agent was gracious enough to enable me to pay the rest upon picking up the tickets.

The week and a half of waiting seemed like eternity, especially when considering that in Wisconsin during that time of year the blizzards (and I don't mean the ice cream kind) may be quite hazardous, and one could get snowed in or iced in for a week. When the day came to leave, the temperature was just above freezing and the air only slightly foggy.

Memories of the night before danced through my mind as I traveled on the bus from Madison to Chicago. The worship, prayers and fellowship all seemed to have had a special anointing, as the community sent me off in the joy of the Lord. I was also thankful that Chicago's O'Hare field was a very familiar place to me by now.

# Return to the Land

# Twelve

# Back in the Land

Landing in Ben Gurion Airport in the late afternoon, I was greeted by the same feelings that I had upon my other two arrivals. *Home sweet home!*

I quickly made my way to a Jerusalem bus stop and purposely stayed away from the taxi drivers, who were shouting out and beckoning with their arms and hands to would-be passengers.

Rather than take chances with some insane driver who would be raring to set a speed record on the Tel Aviv – Jerusalem highway, I preferred standing in the rain waiting for a bus.

As the Jerusalem bound bus rounded one of the last corners, the lights of the city set on a hill were spectacular; they almost seemed like a spray of fireworks dazzling the night sky.

Getting off at the crowded central bus station, I had considered going again to the YMCA for the night, and in the morning calling Sal and Linda, who were settled in a Jerusalem apartment. But as I was coming out of the station, I heard my name being called. I turned and saw a young man and a woman whom I recognized as members of the Project Kibbutz program.

After some greetings and answering their questions, they suggested that I come with them to Art's (the Project's coordinator) home for a meeting with Derek Prince. They also mentioned that it might be possible to stay over there for the night. After a quick phone conversation with Art's wife, Claudia, we were all on our way.

I do not remember the topic of discussion that night, but at one point the phone rang. Claudia came back into the meeting beaming with the good news that two kibbutzim in the North were willing to accept Project volunteers.

My ears perked up when I heard that, as I remembered my hunch about the kibbutzim there, which I voiced to Art during my previous visit.

## An Apartment in Jerusalem

The following day I called Sal and Linda, and to my surprise they told me that they were going away for a few months and needed someone to stay in their apartment. They invited me to stay with them, even prior to their departure, which both gave me a home and some wonderful fellowship.

The two of them were just finishing up a five-days-a-week Hebrew course. I too signed up for such a course, but had to wait a month or so before a new class would start. During that time I ran into Claudia, who told me that Art was in the States recruiting for the following year's program, which was to begin at the end of August.

In almost the same breath she invited me to come with her and four others, to visit the two kibbutzim in the North. The following day I found myself heading north to Kibbutz Gadot and Kibbutz Hulata in the Hula Valley, by the Jordan River and the Golan Heights.

As we drove through the gate and down the driveway of Gadot, I thought I was having a Damascus Road visitation. I was overwhelmed by a powerful encounter with the Holy Spirit. It may have happened in the same place where Saul of Tarsus had his experience. Wherever it was, I turned to Nick, who was to lead the group due to be coming there, and shared with him that "God was going to really anoint this place and move here in a powerful way." Little did I know that this was the very Kibbutz which dismissed, for their faith, the family I had met a year before in Rosh Pina.

In spite of my excitement about Kibbutz Gadot and the area, enrolling in the discipleship-training program for a year held no great fascination. The rules and regulations seemed a little too confining and restrictive for a thirty four year old bachelor. Being under the leadership of some very young people was also not appealing. So, as far as I was concerned the idea of joining Project Kibbutz was not something I was about to consider.

## A Lifetime Challenge

The Ulpan (Hebrew language school) started. Sal and Linda had already left for the States and the challenge of my life was about to begin.

Thankfully Sal and Linda equipped me with many tips about the Ulpan. In my enthusiasm, I had been listening faithfully to a study tape and had also memorized the letters of the alphabet in order to get a head start, which within the very first week was no longer of any benefit, as the pace of studies was very fast.

I was up early for the first school day, eager to catch my bus. Nervous excitement flowed through my veins as the teacher greeted the students. There were about twenty-eight of us, mostly from English speaking countries, a fact, which as it turned out, was not to our benefit, as we conversed in English in between classes.

Each student was asked to introduce himself or herself and state where he or she was from. When I presented myself as Ralph, the teacher gave me funny look, and then asked if I didn't mind taking on a more Hebrew sounding name.

Recalling the time I met that lady who was so

emphatic about my name "having to be" Ephraim, I agreed to be so named in class. Thus, during the three and a half months of the course duration I was known in the Ulpan as "Ephraim," but Ralph elsewhere.

I put my heart and soul into learning the language, but found that the five hours of intensive study in class and the additional five hours of homework were still not enough for me.

Day after day I was getting further behind. Embarrassed to the bone by mental power outs, I was dying daily. The teacher would say something to me, and I could not even get the words out of my mouth to answer her. At other times I could not understand what she was asking me, or what she was saying to the class. But I did do well in grammar and reading.

At one point the teacher took note of my special problem, and having pity on me she did not make me talk in class unless I wanted to, but did encourage me in my stronger areas.

Coming up one day with a novel idea for me to learn the language, she proposed that I associate and play with toddlers and young children. Being a special education teacher I understood the wisdom embedded in that suggestion.

On the streets and in the stores I often embarrassed myself, as I would try and use some simple phrases such as, "How much?" and "Where is it?"

One day I went into a shop to buy a foam mattress. As I was standing next to a stack of mattresses of varying sizes, the proprietor came over to me and asked if he could help. Pointing to one of the foam pieces, I asked him quite confidently: *"Ma ha'sha'a'?"* When he responded with a puzzled look I realized that what I had said was, "what is the time?"

Quite often people would simply lose patience when trying to make out what I was trying to say and would ask me politely to speak English to them, thus also taking advantage of an opportunity to brush up their English.

I must have had one of the largest English practice classes in all of Israel!

Being alone in the apartment was nice, as there was very little interference in my studies. One day, however, a Believer from South Africa moved into the apartment next door. After getting to know one another, we would arise early, and pray and study the Scriptures together. Many of the Old Testament Prophets spoke to us in a very personal way, touching our hearts deeply and confirming that we were in the right place at the right time. However, neither one of us was sure how he was going to be able to stay in the Land.

Johann eventually helped start the International Christian Embassy, and became its first president. I, on the other hand, became a "Kibbutznik," but not right there and then. The Lord was faithful to answer our prayers, and both of us were surprised at how He managed to lead us to our respective destinies.

## A Kingdom Song

It was around 5:00 a.m., August 12, 1978, when I woke up extra early with the lyrics of a song buzzing in my head. I got up and began to write down the words. The more I wrote the more words came. Finally I completed the task and fit the words to the tune of a Bob Dylan song called "Mister Tambourine Man."

The song went something like this:

Chorus:
The Kingdom of God is at hand,
Calling out a people in His Land;
Walking in the way of the light of the truth,
Being the ripeness of first fruit.
Verse One:
I'm calling out a people for My name sake,

Calling them to pray, calling them to praise,
Calling them to walk in My ways, in My ways...for...
Chorus
Verse Two:
I'm calling out a people, who will stand by my side,
Will not compromise; will not fall aside;
People who will stand and will know, and will
know...that...
Chorus
Verse Three:
I'm calling out a people, who will stand and say "No,"
To the Devil and all God's foes, to the pride Satan has
chose;
A people who will stay and will not go, will not
go...for...
Chorus
Verse Four:
Yes, He's calling out a people for His name sake,
Returning this earth, giving new birth;
Returning the Kingdom of God to this world, to this
world...
Chorus

## Kibbutz Life

The Ulpan class was coming to an end for me and it
seemed that I was a lost cause, even though I was one of
the remaining 12 students out of the original 28 who
started. That in itself was no small achievement. Many
students started over again, something that I too had
considered doing. However, a friend of mine from
Monterey, California, who had come to the Land a few
months beforehand, and who was volunteering on a
kibbutz in the Western Galilee, was starting to plant
other thoughts into my mind. I had been to visit him a
few times, and he had asked me if I would join him as a
fellow volunteer. I was beginning to like the idea of

trying out kibbutz life, but was concerned about my age, since I knew that many kibbutzim had an age limit for volunteers.

Around that same time, I ran into a somewhat anxious Art Carlson in Jerusalem, who did not have a male leader for one of the groups in a Jerusalem area kibbutz. He asked me to pray about joining the program and about taking that leadership position. I still could not see myself in such a discipleship program, especially not in leadership, not having gone through the program myself. So I passed up the opportunity.

Some time went by and I had no idea what the next step was to be. One early morning, I suddenly felt an urge to go and visit my friend in the Western Galilee kibbutz. I had to go first to the seacoast town of Nahariya, and from there, catch a bus to the kibbutz. Upon arriving at the volunteer quarters I inquired about Mark, only to find out that he had left the kibbutz that morning, heading for Jerusalem. I had assumed then that he was coming to visit me, although he had not made any previous arrangements.

Then my informant told me that Mark had left permanently and was going home. Shocked, I returned immediately to Jerusalem and found Mark waiting for me. My idea of going to that kibbutz suddenly came to a screeching halt.

## A Change of Plans

Mark stayed with me for about a week, until he found a flight back to the States. Sal and Linda were due back about the same time with their dog, so I knew that I would have to find other accommodations. Kibbutz seemed now the only option.

So one day I got on a bus and went out to Art's home. In some way I felt that I was traveling in a direction opposite to where I really wanted to go. Being a man of faith, I put out a fleece. If Art would be at home, I bargained, it would be a sign that I was to join Project Kibbutz, whether I liked it or not.

As I was looking out the bus window, I thought I saw Art's van going into town. "Well, I guess that puts an end to the PK idea," I told myself.

Arriving at Art's house, indeed the van was not to be seen, but who should open the door for me but Art?

Apparently one of the volunteers had borrowed the vehicle in order to pick up some supplies.

I wasted no time in asking him if the position he had mentioned to me a while back was still open.

He immediately said that it was, but at the same time discerned my reservation, and so added, "Let's go into the living room and pray."

After a few minutes of prayer, Art looked up at me and said, "Actually Ralph, any of the kibbutzim are open for you to go to."

"Even Kibbutz Gadot?" I asked, surprised at my own response.

"Sure," he said, "I will be going up there in a couple of days and you can pack your belongings and come along."

Joy filled my being, as I felt that the Lord was directing my path. I could not wait to tell Sal and Linda, who were due to return the following day.

This wonderful couple had all their belongings and their dog with them when they came through the door.

We had a lot to share with one another, so the time went by fast. At the end of these two days Art picked me up and I was on my way to a new adventure in the Land of my forefathers.

# Thirteen

# A New Adventure

The Hula valley, at the base of the Golan Heights and Mount Hermon, is a very picturesque area of northern Israel. I was happy to be there, even though a cyclone fence topped with three strands of barb wire all the way around surrounded the kibbutz.

By the time of my arrival, the others who were enrolled in PK had already been on the kibbutz for a couple of weeks and had time to get to know one another. Nick, one of the leaders, escorted me to my room and introduced me to my roommate.

"Ralph, I would like you to meet Ralph."

The two Ralphs were sitting on their beds talking, when someone shouted from the outside: "Hey Ralph, come quickly!"

We both shot to our feet. At that moment I realized that this was not going to work. I told Ralph to call me Ephraim, as I had gotten used to that name in the Ulpan. "Besides," I thought to myself, "he was more a Ralph type than me..." So from then on everyone nick-named me Ephraim, Ephi or Froike, and had I become too spiritual, I would have been in danger of being called *"Freakie Froike Frank."*

The living arrangements for the eleven of us in PK were not the most glamorous. As a matter of fact, our accommodations were the "has-been" volunteer quarters of a quarter of a century past. These buildings were actually portable cement rooms, with wood chip boards for internal walls. The holes and broken areas allowed the mice, rats and cockroaches to scamper back and forth without too much of a problem.

One night, as I was lying on my bed, a rat stuck its head out of a hole just above me. He did not seem to be intimidated by my presence, and ventured out on the shelf just above my head. He must have thought that he could grab the candy bar that was there and beat it back to the hole before I could do anything about it. However, the little critter had one problem, the candy was heavier than expected and so he and the sweet chocolate ended up on my pillow. I jumped up about as fast as he came down. Escaping was not a problem for him, as there were plenty of passageways to run through.

## Welding?

For the first few weeks I was assigned, along with most of the volunteers, to pick grapefruit. But because of our protracted stay, permanent work places were to be allocated for the PK volunteers. One day, upon arriving back from the fields, there was a note on the door that I was to go to the *"mas'geria"* the following day.

No one seemed to know what that was, and what's more I could hardly pronounce this strange word. That evening in the communal dinning room the Volunteer Coordinator told me that it meant "welding shop."

*"Welding!* I thought to myself, *"I had attempted it once, many years ago, and am sure that the electrode I used is still stuck to the metal to this very day."*

With a look of compassion on his face, the man told me not to be intimidated by my prospective boss, whom no one could get along with and hence was not very much in demand as a work partner. With that encouragement I hardly slept that night. Everyone was praying for me as

I made my way to work the next morning.

The sun was not up yet when I walked into the building (or shed) which housed the welding shop. My new boss was standing next to an electric kettle that had just boiled. I greeted him and for a second thought that he wasn't going to respond. Then, in broken English, he said "Good morning" and "Would you like some coffee?"

I answered, "Just hot water for me, thanks."

It was then that I got a good look at the stocky, goateed man with one glass-eye.

"Just hot water?!" His glance told me that, had he known my name, he no doubt would have called me Freakie Froike Frank.

I, for my part, watched him put into his small cup two heaping teaspoons of Turkish coffee and three teaspoons of sugar, rendering that cup half full even before the water was poured into it. After adding the water, my new boss stirred it a couple of times and walked off.

I wondered whether he had gone to get some metal shavings to add to his drink.

In a few minutes he returned, took his cup and began to sip off the black liquid that floated above the thick mud-like substance.

He watched me very carefully as I sipped my hot water, and I did the same while he sipped his drink. "Sobol is my name," he said, breaking the silence.

"I'm Ephraim," I answered.

"Ah, Froike!" he responded back.

I didn't know it at the time, but there were two or three other Ephraims on the kibbutz. Sobol must have thought it more convenient to pin me with a nickname right away.

I spent the entire work time with brooms, brushes and shovels cleaning the place, and by the end of the day I was as black from the metal dust and dirt as was Sobol's coffee.

We didn't talk much, as he spent most of the time

conversing with others who came in and out of the shop.

When I was about to retire to my living quarters, Sobol turned to me and said: " I see you like to work, I'm going in to the Work Coordinator and see if I can get you assigned to this place. Can you weld?"

"No," I answered.

"Well, I'll teach you" Sobol promised, confident that he could convince the work committee to allow him to have me as a full-time worker for the entire year.

His confidence was not unfounded, as he had a reputation for throwing chairs and tables around if he didn't get his way. And indeed, the following day I was told that I would be assigned to the welding shop.

I caught on quickly to the instructions, and within a short time I knew how to use all the machines and welding equipment. I then remembered the dream I had about the barrel that contained the different types of seed, and that God had told me that I would be doing something in the Land that I had never done before. This must have been it.

## No Dating?

Bible studies, Scripture memorization, prayer meetings, general meetings, and Hebrew language classes were all part of the PK program. That is, after an eight-hour day of work.

Many times during the prayer meetings I would go into deep contemplation. Unfortunately, when I started snoring, the others frowned on my form of meditation.

One of the main rules of the program was no dating. This rule eliminated any need for marriage counseling. Nevertheless, our boy and girl leaders fell in love after three months, and so had to leave the program.

Another young lady took on the roll of girl leader, and I was voted in to be the boy leader. I was thankful that we had some fairly mature people in our group, as that reduced a lot of the problems that other groups had. It did not, however, do away with the boy-girl pairing-off phenomenon and with the relationships that were being formed. There was even some behind-the-back holding of hands that almost got our group disbanded and sent home.

Being a good Christian group, love was in the air, and kibbutz life style lent to the atmosphere. I too fell victim to an insidious, infectious infatuation.

The kibbutz members, by the way, thought it rather strange that this natural process was so strictly forbidden, especially when you're over thirty.

## Cliff and Cliff

When I first arrived, I was warned about a young American Jew who had come to volunteer, primarily to be able to finish writing a book that could only be defined as "filthy."

Cliff was not able to utter a sentence without cursing or swearing. He must have pronounced Jesus' name, with or without Christ, more than all of us put together.

When he was in college, he took it upon himself to harass campus evangelists and tried to pit Christians against one another doctrinally.

Having heard that I had Jewish blood, his harassment of me was intensified. He used to greet me in the dining room with bellows of, "You traitor."

Fortunately, it didn't bother me. God actually gave me a love for this guy and we became friends. He loved to discuss philosophy and so did I. At times we would talk for hours. But for some reason we never discussed Christianity, probably because he already knew most of the doctrines.

In our talks I focused mainly on the faith of our common ancestor, Abraham, and on his relationship with the God of Israel.

There were a couple of atheist kibbutz members who had emigrated from the United States, and after talking with me, Cliff would go over to them.

These ongoing cycles went on for about six months, until one Friday night...

Around midnight, someone showed up at the kibbutz gate.  He was stranded on the Golan Heights and couldn't get back to town,  so he made his way to our kibbutz.

The Volunteer Coordinator was summoned to let the stranger in, and he asked Cliff if the stranded individual could spend the night in his room.

It turned out that both these now roommates had the same first and last names.  Cliff, the stranger, was also a writer, who just happened to be a Believer.

On Sunday, Cliff from the kibbutz, stopped by my workplace and told me that he had been led to accept Jesus as his Jewish Messiah.  Within a few weeks he immersed himself in the Jordan River.

As that year the water level was very low because of drought, he needed help in order to be fully immersed. Amazingly, our God must have given him a new language, as when Cliff came out, he never used another foul word again

## Spring is in the Air

Periodically, PK had arranged for the two northern groups to have seminars with visiting speakers. This took place either on Gadot or Hulata. On this particular weekend our group was to host the Hulata group, in addition to author and minister, Art Katz.

Art Katz was accompanied by a fellow about my age, who was an artist and had become a Believer a month or so before coming to Israel.  Allen was Jewish, and he loved the kibbutz and stayed on as a volunteer.

One day, on my way to a leadership meeting in

Hulata, I invited him to come along. It was a beautiful spring day, so we took our time walking through the orchards and cotton fields of the two kibbutzim. The beauty that only the eyes of an artist could appreciate overwhelmed Allen.

Upon our arrival in Hulata, we happened to run into one of the PK volunteers. What took place after I introduced Al to Julie, who was a former airline stewardess, should not have been deemed unexpected, but natural.

Lo and behold, PK had another problem on its hands.

The infectious disease that we called "LAFS," had spread from Gadot to Hulata! It was a common, though not easily curable condition, better known as "Love At First Sight."

With another six months to go, we were not sure we would make it through to the end. The incredible and beautifully garlanded hills and valleys, with their multiple colored flowers, did not make it any easier to abide by the rules.

The landscape was a fitting courting ground for lovebirds, and as mentioned, I too was overcome by strong feelings for a much younger lady in our group.

This resulted in Art and his PK assistant coming to pay all of us a very serious visit. They had received information from my counterpart in leadership concerning some "hanky-panky" that had been going on.

Art was not happy and was ready to send all of us back home, but in the end left us with a warning that we were not to be seen even holding hands.

As one of the leaders, I had to enforce this edict.

The months went by, and most of us, at least publicly, abided by the rules.

After the year was over and all the others returned to their countries of origin, including my girlfriend, I was feeling very strongly to stay on as a volunteer, but this time not as part of Project Kibbutz. The kibbutz authorities, however, denied my request.

# Return to the Land

My boss, who really wanted me to stay, as we had become good friends, and worked well together in the course of the year, came up with a possible solution.

Sobol went to the main office and requested that I be granted permission to remain on as a volunteer until the Absorption Committee would decide whether I could apply as a candidate for membership.

## A Change of Status

After a few weeks, word came that the committee would not consider the request, as I was not Jewish. They recommended that I apply instead to the Social Committee.

During my short interview with the Committee members I was asked about my Christianity. My answer was that I did not believe in the Protestant-Catholic expression. They then asked me if I would go through conversion to the Jewish religion, to which I responded that it would be quite hypocritical, as the kibbutz itself was not religious, and thus I would not be able to adhere to all the demands placed upon a convert. I don't think these "chaverim" ("members" and/or "friends," the term commonly used for kibbutz residents) really understood either of my answers, as their English was not that good. Ultimately both committees refused to recommend my candidacy.

Sobol, however, understanding the kibbutz procedures, told me that there was still another alternative. He himself could recommend me to the general assembly, which would then vote on my case, although, without the approval of the two committees, that mode of action was very unlikely to succeed.

I agreed with Sobol and believed in Proverbs 16:9: "A man's heart plan his way, but the Lord directs his steps."

Sobol requested that my case be placed on the agenda of the upcoming general meeting.   When the big day finally arrived, tension was in the air.

People were discussing the forthcoming meeting, but I was not permitted to participate in the debate. However, I was later given a blow-by-blow description of the evening's proceedings by some of my friends.

The issue of my candidacy led to a discussion on the ideology of the Kibbutz Movement. That was the only topic that was discussed through that stormy meeting, which lasted from 9:00 p.m. to 2:00 a.m. and beyond.

When the smoke had cleared and the hands were counted, I was voted in as a candidate. I would have that status for two years, before I could apply for membership. Some of my close friends told me that they voted against me, not because they objected to me personally, but because one of their primary reasons for living in this type of community was for the purpose of welcoming Jewish immigration into Israel.

Another reason for the intense arguments, even among good friends, was that a couple of years before my case had come up, a family was voted off the kibbutz for professing their belief in Yeshua as the Jewish Messiah. Apparently that case became a divisive issue among the members, and many wounds had not been healed by the time my case came to the fore. It had been two years since I had met these very people in Rosh Pina at the house of the two brothers.

*Above)* Kibbutz Gadot
flanked by snow capped Hermon range.
*Below)* Singing with Project Kibbutz volunteers.

## Fourteen

# A Bus Ride and "Ph"

During this time, I had been corresponding quite seriously with my girlfriend in the States, and thought that perhaps she might return to the kibbutz. Alan and Julie, however, wasted no time after their return to the States. The two of them got married right away and came back to Israel as new immigrants and moved to Jerusalem, where they were residing in an Absorption Center for new immigrants in the neighborhood of Gilo. In late spring of that year I remembered that I had not used my open-ended, one-year ticket to the States, which was issued two years earlier. So, in hopes of being able to redeem the ticket, I traveled from the kibbutz to TWA's main office in Jerusalem. Arriving with my little red backpack at the now quite familiar Central Bus Station in Jerusalem, within minutes I caught a bus to the downtown area where the TWA office was located.

## A Chance Encounter

Unbeknown to me there was a female passenger on that bus, who had an altogether different experience during that short ten minute ride. While on that same bus and being in a hurry to get home, as it was Friday noon and public transportation was about to cease, and the shops to shut down shortly, her attention was drawn to an American looking man with a red backpack who had boarded the bus at the Central Bus Station. As the bus proceeded down the street toward the downtown area, she was suddenly struck with a strong feeling to share the gospel with him. However, being a Believer for only one month she was reluctant to get up and approach a stranger in this manner.

Many thoughts flooded her mind: "Am I being disobedient to the Lord?" And, "Perhaps he already knows the Lord, in which case he may show up the following day at the Baptist Assembly meeting," which she was about to attend for the second time only, for a special Pentecost service.

The bus slowed to one of the stops, and the American disembarked. Suddenly a very strange sensation came over her, it was as though her whole being was cut asunder, to be followed instantly by a thought that flashed across her mind like a neon light:

*"You have just been severed from your other half."*

Back home, she suddenly felt that she knew that the man's name had an "f" sounding consonant in it, but which was spelled with a "ph."

As for me, I stayed overnight with Alan and Julie and on the following day, while in town, I visited some friends. In the late morning I decided to go over to the Baptist House, where the meeting was almost over. As I was about to leave, Zippora, the lady who had insisted that I take the name Ephraim, walked up to me.

We chatted for a few minutes and then she pointed over to a couple of women she was with. I glanced over but could not make out any one person. One of the two women was the one who was on the bus the day before.

After Zippora and I parted, this woman approached Zippora and asked her about the man that she had seen her talking to. She would have come over and introduced herself if she were not in a hurry for a previously made appointment. "He is a sweet brother from the Galilee," was Zippora's answer. But that did not suffice.

"What is his name?" was the next question.

The answer took her by surprise, "His name is Ephraim in Hebrew, and Ralph in English."

Not only was there a *ph* in the first name, but there was another one in the second!

## The Engagement Ring

I, of course was not party to any of this, and walked from the Baptist House down to the Old City where I hired an Arab taxi to take me back up to the kibbutz, as there were no buses running on Shabbat.

The airlines agreed to honor the ticket whenever I decided to go back to the States, so with my mission accomplished, I settled back into the routines of everyday life on the kibbutz.

Pam (my friend in the States) and I were writing each other quite frequently and discussing possible timing for a wedding. It was about then that I received a letter from the woman in Idabel, Oklahoma, whom I had briefly ministered to three years before. It was in the envelope of that letter that she had placed her engagement ring.

At the time I thought perhaps this was a confirmation that Pam and I would get engaged. However, for some reason I never told her about the ring. Besides, it seemed much too small for her fingers. I slipped the ring into its small envelope and placed it in my Bible

## Meeting Rimona

During the Fall Feasts that year I received a holiday greeting card from Julie and Alan, who had changed his name to Elchanan. The card included an invitation to come up to visit them. They wanted to introduce me to a lady named Rimona, whom they had just met at a home fellowship in Gilo. Apparently she had recently moved to an apartment across from the Absorption Center, where she lived on her own.

One day, after coming home from work to the empty apartment she thought she heard the name "Frank" resonating off the walls. Puzzled by this, she was wondering if this was not a sign that a person by that name, whom she had known since her youth, was on his way to Israel from his native England, and on his way to meeting his Messiah.

At the end of that fellowship meeting in Gilo, Julie and Elchanan were exchanging testimonies with this new neighbor of theirs. She told them that before she became a Believer she had been involved in a cult group. Julie listened, then turned to Elchanan and asked him if this was the same cult that Ephraim Frank had been in.

Without as much as taking a breath, she turned back to Rimona and told her about this friend that they had on a kibbutz up in the Galilee.

Rimona, putting two and two together, proceeded to tell them about the experience that she had on the bus. It was then that she learned that the name "Frank," that she had heard almost audibly reverberating off her apartment's walls, was the last name of this mysterious Ephraim-Ralph, whom she had seen on the bus and at the Baptists' House several months before.

I was not particularly interested in meeting this Rimona, as I had Pam on my mind. I therefore did not respond to Julie's invitation.

## The Name Becomes Official

Three months later I was entertaining quite seriously the thought of going back to the States to get more of my belongings and to visit Pam. So I went to Tel Aviv to renew my passport and to have my new name added to it. And because the kibbutz had been doing all the paper work in the name Ephraim, I thought it best to contact my parents and have them officially add the name to my birth certificate.

From Tel Aviv it was only a short ride to Jerusalem. There, I would visit Elchanan and Julie, and perhaps meet Rimona as well. However, she had taken a trip to Europe, and as it turned out she spent half her time sick in bed. During that time, when she was incapacitated and lying in bed in Zurich, Rimona heard in her spirit that this Ephraim had another woman in his life.

It was therefore no great surprise to her when she returned home to learn of this fact from Julie (who up until that time had not made her privy to this information).

Spring was now in the air. The flowers were in full bloom in the Galilee when Julie called me and said that they were coming up to the kibbutz for a weekend, and were bringing Rimona with them.

I was at work when they arrived, and happened to be driving by on a tractor when I saw them walking in. I was not that impressed by the lady with the pigtails and 'hippy' style dress, who was introduced to me from a distance. I hurriedly told my guests that I would meet them in the dining hall for lunch and drove away.

That afternoon I took off work early so that I could entertain my visitors, and after the meal in the dinning hall, I invited them over for some homemade snacks.

When Rimona walked into my kibbutz apartment, she immediately spotted on the door of my refrigerator a sign that said "one and one makes one" and on the top of the small cooler a stack of wedding photos (of Becky and Steward, two of the love birds who met on our P K team). Pam, who was Becky's bride's maid, had sent them to me.

Walking past the kitchen and into my little living room, Rimona recognized the upholstery as being the same as what she had before her last move, as well as the posters on the walls that were identical to the ones she found in her Gilo apartment. Since my desert-making skills did not extend beyond granola cheese cake, I offered that to my company, and it so happened that some of Rimona's favorite foods were granola *and* cheesecake.

Later that evening, I gave her a book to read, which she took with her to the room she was occupying.

Without realizing it, a bookmark that I had inserted in it was still there. It happened to be a bridal consultant's business card.

While all these little signs were coming Rimona's way, I myself was not seeing stars, and as a matter of fact, remained quite indifferent.

The following day the four of us, or maybe I should say five, as Julie was very pregnant, took a car from the kibbutz up to Tel Dan, which is a very beautiful spot at the headwater of the Jordan River.

It was a very special day with the multi colored flowers gracing the landscape, interesting archeological sites like that of an old water mill, which we visited, and of course, the famous ice cold river water.

When we got back, we were all quite tired after tramping and touring. That evening Elchanan and Julie went back to Jerusalem, but Rimona stayed over night.

I, of course, started work very early the next day and later met my guest for breakfast. I then drove her the very short distance that separated the kibbutz from the main highway, so that she could catch a bus back to Jerusalem. Rimona and I parted with a quick Christian hug and with, *"See you around."*

## See You Around?

My cool and noncommittal parting comment was anything but heartwarming for Rimona.

She felt as if there was no substance, or even a sign of friendship, expressed in our departure. Boarding the bus she was very disappointed, thinking to herself, *"He didn't even ask for my telephone number. Is this all that this was coming to...?"*

After nine months of so many clear signs pointing out this man, including the time just spent with him on the kibbutz, she did not know what to think.

As she was boarding the almost packed-to-capacity bus, her ears caught a song playing on the radio, with a message to the effect that life was not in our hands to handle, and that we just needed to wait things out.

With tears in her eyes she sat down on the steps next to the door. As she looked up, she saw, in the dust and dirt of the window, words that were nonchalantly scribbled there, but which to her were of special significance at that moment, "I love you."

Arriving at the Tiberius bus station, someone from the depot had yelled out to the driver: "Where is Yehoshua?" (Joshua), pronouncing the name like "Yeshua." To which the diver's response was, "He's coming soon!" Each of these little happenings brought with it the comforting embrace of her Messiah.

## Still Oblivious...

In the meantime I returned to work, as if nothing of import had happened, other than a nice visit from some friends. Pam and I continued to correspond and were looking forward to my visit to the States.

I had now been a candidate for almost a year and half, at which time Sobol and his Danish wife decided to go for a year to Denmark.

Their departure left me fully in charge of the welding shop, which kept me busy with the demands of fixing farming equipment, building and repairing everything and anything that was made of metal and used on the kibbutz.

The Work Committee allowed me to have a helper, a youth named Shai, who was waiting for his recruitment into the army. He was a good worker, but liked to goof around a lot. He also loved photography and looked at his welding more as form of art than as a job.

Another kibbutz member named Jerome, an

Ethiopian who had converted to Judaism, worked periodically in the shop too.

Having the responsibility of being in charge of a branch (as each work area is called on the kibbutz), was very helpful toward being accepted as a full-fledged member.

The time of my candidacy was drawing to an end, so I requested six weeks off to go to the States in order to bring back my belongings that were stored at my parents' house in Wisconsin. I informed Pam that I would be coming out to visit her in Idaho.

The time of departure had arrived and I, of course, took the opportunity to visit with Elchanan and Julie in Jerusalem.

It so happened that on the evening of my arrival some Believers were gathering in their home. I met some old friends, as well as a number of new people. Rimona was also there, but I did not say much more than "Hi" to her during the entire evening.

I spent almost the whole time talking to an American woman who was a recent immigrant to Israel and whom I had met one time before, while living in Jerusalem.

I did, however, walk Rimona home after the meeting. At one point during the five-minute journey, she asked me point plank if God had been showing me anything in regards to her. I was a little taken aback, but answered her with a very frank, "No," which brought an end to the conversation.

## Fifteen

# Uprooted and Replanted

As the taxi took me the next day to the airport, my mind was occupied with the situation in the believing community in Wisconsin, which met at my older sister's home. There had been a big split there over some doctrines of the faith movement. It would not have been so bad had it not involved my two sisters and their husbands, each being on different ends of the controversy. Both sides had been asking me for my opinion on the matter. But having been outside the American Charismatic evolution for a couple of years, I did not really know what I was getting into, except that people who used to support one another lovingly were no longer talking to each other.

Sitting in my friends' living room the previous night, I had been looking through a book on embryonic development that was lying on the coffee table, as Julie was now only a few weeks away from giving birth. Being a Biology major, I was familiar with the topic.

As I paused to look closely at the pictures of the chromosomes and the cellular division, which takes place in the growing process, I suddenly remembered a film I had watched in college, or on TV, on this very subject.

While nicely lined up and peacefully harmonizing with one another, the chromosomes suddenly begin to vibrate and shake before the "big bang" of division takes place. At that point, they go in opposite directions until they polarize, and another cell is formed with a wall dividing the two. This natural part of the growing process results, eventually, in a new human being.

Pondering this amazing process helped me understand what had taken place in our community. Even though it looked and felt terrible while it was happening, it was an inevitable part of the process of growth.

Armed with that insight, I arrived in Wisconsin after being away for three years. Once in that familiar setting, it did not seem more than a day had gone by. However, one there was one surprise: Pam was there to greet me!

Although things did not seem quite the same as when she was in Israel, we did spend that week together, after which she returned to Idaho. We made arrangements for me to join her there, after my quick stop in California.

While in Monterey, it was good to meet up with my friends again. The night before flying to see Pam, I had dreamed that I was in a car driven by someone else, and that we had come to a barricade in the road with flashing yellow lights. The friend (with whom I had been staying in California) was standing in front of the barricade waving his arms and motioning to us to stop, as the road had apparently given way and there was a huge drop-off on the other side. I felt that the dream may have had something to do with the trip to Idaho, but that remained to be seen later.

## Not Going Anywhere

Pam and her mother picked me at the airport. Pam's mother and I were almost the same age, which added to the already existing feeling of awkwardness. Indeed, as the days of my stay went by, it was becoming obvious that this relationship was not going anywhere.

As a matter of fact, the last night, just before leaving on a train, during a little farewell party that Pam's mother threw for me, Pam herself had disappeared.

Later on her mother had to take me to the train station. She was very apologetic about her daughter's behavior and disclosed to me that Pam had spent most of the evening with her boy friend.

## He Was Still in Charge

Joy shot through my soul like a lightening bolt. I felt free and thankful to the Lord that in spite of my decisions, He still directed my path.

Traveling on the train was an extra special treat, as the sunrise brought with it the incredible scenery of the State of Montana. A large bull moose was standing near a creek that fed a lush green valley, with snow-capped mountains forming the background. I thought I was in paradise!

Arriving back in Wisconsin, I soon had a dozen confirmations that the relationship with Pam was not what the Father had planned for me. The dream I had at my friend's house seemed quite obvious, now that I was looking at it in hindsight.

So once again I said goodbye to family and friends, and taking my belongings in two large heavy suitcases, I was on my way back to the Land.

## My Fourth Planting

This was now the fourth time that I was making my way back to Israel. But something seemed very different about this trip; perhaps it was because I knew that this little seed (me) of Jacob was no longer going to be sifted here and there among the nations, but was coming home to be planted into the ground. This feeling revived in me an indelible memory of a special moment that I had experienced in my first year on the kibbutz.

While working in the metal shop one day, a large John Deer tractor with a six-bottom plow came in to be repaired; one of its main support beams cracked and had to be welded. As I was kneeling down on the cement, beneath this instrument of the soil, a large chunk of that rich Hula valley earth fell and broke in front of me. I stopped welding, and when I glanced at it an indescribable love welled up inside of me. I broke into tears, as a Scripture raced through my mind:

"You shall no longer be labeled forsaken, nor shall your land any more be termed desolate; but you shall be called Hephzibah, and your land Beulah; for the Lord delights in you, and your land shall be married; for as a young man marries a virgin, so shall your sons marry you" (Isaiah 62:4-5, NKJV).

This again was one of those embarrassing moments, as I held the welding mask in front of my face to keep the plowman from seeing me cry.

## Welcome Home!

Arriving at Ben Gurion Airport on that hot mid morning of July 1981, I was welcomed by a number of taxi drivers who were more than anxious to take me to my destination. I addressed the driver who approached me in English, stating that I would like to go to the Tel-Aviv central bus station, as I had planned to take a bus from there to the Galilee.

The driver lifted my two very heavy suitcases into the trunk of his car, and upon my asking, told me what the fare would be. It sounded reasonable enough.

Suddenly an English speaking couple that looked like newlyweds, approached him and inquired about the fare to Tel Aviv. The price he quoted was much higher than what he told me. Upon overhearing this exchange, I said in Hebrew that it was way over the necessary amount. I said the same to the couple, but in English.

The taxi driver was furious. "Why did you speak to me in English when you can speak Hebrew?" he shouted very loudly. He then walked over to the trunk, opened it, and flung my suitcases to the ground, continuing to yell: *"Lech lechah! Be gone!"*

I picked up my belongings and strangely enough felt as though I had just been welcomed back to the Land!

Dragging myself along with the suitcases and back-pack, I went to a bus stop that was marked "Tel-Aviv" and "Jerusalem."

Just then a thought came to mind about my friends Julie and Elchanan, whose baby was born while I was in the States. In my mind I gambled, "I will take the first bus that arrives. If it is the Tel-Aviv one, I will return to the kibbutz, and if it is the one going to Jerusalem, I will go and visit Elchanan and Julie and their new baby." The first bus that pulled up was headed for Jerusalem.

## Still Missing My Intended

After checking my suitcases into the storage room of the Jerusalem central bus station, I took bus number 31 and went to Gilo to visit my friends.

That very morning Rimona was planning to go to the dentist and also to attend a prayer meeting afterwards, when a lady friend of hers dropped by to discuss some personal matters and pray. Sensing that was more important than her appointment, she stayed on and listened to her friend.

When the friend left she was still determined to make it to the prayer meeting on time. After running hurriedly across the street to the bus stop and while waiting somewhat anxiously, she was suddenly arrested by a question which popped into her mind: *"Lord, when will You arrange another meeting with this Ephraim?"*

We seemed to run into each other every few months, and she no sooner put the period under the mental question mark, than a bus pulled away from the stop directly across the road, and who should appear out of the dust and smoke issuing from that departing vehicle?

I was making my way across the road to Julie and

Elchanan's, and lo and behold, standing on the sidewalk was none other than Rimona!

Surprised, we greeted each other and together walked over to our mutual friends with whom we spent the afternoon and evening. I left very early the next morning to go back to the kibbutz, but still had no leading or feeling that Rimona was the one made in heaven for me.

## More Jerusalem Adventures

About a month and a half later my niece Julie came to take part in the Project Kibbutz program. Since the kibbutz that she was headed for was close to mine, I thought I would meet her at the airport and have no problem getting a ride back home. So I took the day off and went down to Ben Gurion Airport.

The flight was delayed and arrived much later than anticipated, at around 11:30 p.m. My expectations to go back with the bus rented by the Project were also shattered, as there was no room for me. The public buses had already stopped running, and I did not have enough money for a taxi. Having no other recourse I planned to spend the night in the airport, and turned to walk back inside. As I came to the door, I bumped into a man I had met a couple of times in a Jerusalem congregation.

Although we did not really know each other, we exchanged greetings and our respective reasons for being there. He then invited me to come with him to Jerusalem, and to stay at his mother's apartment. By the time we arrived at her house it was about 1:30 a.m.

As we walked around the corner of a building near her complex, we noticed the police parked outside. Suddenly my companion grabbed me by the arm and jerked me back. Alarmed he said, "We can't go in just now," and he admitted that he was the one the police were looking for.

After the police left, we proceeded to the apartment, only to be greeted by a hysterical mother. She and her son got into a very heated conversation in Hebrew, and finally, at about 2:30 a.m., they gave me a little cot on a balcony. I must have lain awake for about half an hour when the door buzzer went off.

When the mother opened the door the police were standing there. I did not take a breath until they left with her son, and then did not sleep for much more than one hour. It was just before dawn when I packed up, left a "thank you" note and escaped.

Since I was not quite sure which part of town I was in, I started walking downhill until I found myself at the Damascus Gate of the Old City. Locating a park bench, I sat and waited for the sun to come up.

Later, as I was making my way to the Baptist bookstore, which was in the center of town, I chanced to meet my old friends from Rosh Pina in the Galilee. Since they were heading in the same direction, we walked together.

Not finding what they were looking for at the Baptist bookstore, they asked me if I wanted to come with them down to the Bible Society's shop. Although I was thinking about going back to the kibbutz, I decided to spend some time with my old friends, and so tagged along.

At the bookshop, I was surprised to see none other than Rimona busily arranging books on a shelf. Apparently she had been employed there temporarily. By the time we arrived at the store I was about ready to drop, so I contemplated deferring my return to the kibbutz by several hours, and asking Rimona if she would not mind letting me get some sleep in her apartment.

As for Rimona, she too was in for a surprise as she surveyed the train of familiar individuals (another friend had joined us in the meantime) which filed in, with me in the rear. She agreed to my request, and gave me the key to her apartment, but what she did not tell me was that she had a roommate!

I found my way to the apartment, let myself in and discovered the cot that she spoke about in the spare bedroom. After about three or four hours of sleep, I heard someone come in. Assuming it was Rimona, I got up, went to the living room and waited. All at once an unknown woman came out of one of the bedrooms, wearing only a slip.

She took one look at me and I knew I was in trouble. Fumbling for words of explanation and apologies did me no good, as she ran back into her bedroom.

While she stayed locked up, I sat in the living room, still waiting for Rimona. The lady never said a word to me after that, nor did she ever have a kind word to say about me!

## The Tel Dan Waterwheel

Rimona and I said our farewells for the fifth or sixth time now, without any real change in my attitude toward her. But for Rimona these chance meetings were more than happenstance.

At one point, shortly after our first encounter on the kibbutz, one of her believing girlfriends had an impression that the two of them, along with another friend, were to pray together for husbands.

As they were praying, the friend had a vision of an old waterwheel. There was an ancient waterwheel in the only place where the two of us had been together up until that point, and that was the waterwheel in Tel Dan.

During a fellowship service, someone also had a vision of Rimona as a pearl on top of a mountain. Hours before she felt as if the Father was allowing her to eavesdrop on a conversation that He was having with me. "I am preparing for you a gem of a wife," was what she heard Him say.

And when, in the course of the meeting, everyone sang, "This mountain shall be removed," it was the obstacle of "Mount Ephraim" that she was thinking of.

The vision that she was presented with was therefore a great encouragement to her.

## Sixteen

# The Wind of the Spirit

Wedding bells were ringing for a friend of mine who had come to our kibbutz earlier in the year. He had been asked to leave the kibbutz he was on because of his faith, but on Kibbutz Gadot he met another Jewish Believer, and both were now candidates for membership.

One day as Gary and I were traveling together to Haifa, he asked me about Rimona and our relationship. He had known her from his interim days in Jerusalem, before coming to Gadot, and was very emphatic about my need to spend some quality time with her, if indeed God was bringing her into my life.

Heeding my friend's advice, I called Rimona and invited her to come to the kibbutz for a weekend. She arrived on a Friday afternoon in the beginning of December. We did some visiting with Gary and his wife, then went to the Shabbat-eve meal in the dining hall.

Afterwards, at my apartment, we spent many hours talking about our "non-relationship." The conversation was really going nowhere, and by the end of it, Rimona was quite frustrated.

At one point she told me that there seemed to be some kind of an impenetrable wall, or barrier, between us. We parted that evening without any change in sight.

During the night Rimona decided that she would somehow find a ride and leave the next morning, even though it was Shabbat, as it appeared that there was nothing more to discuss.

She awoke just before dawn and was pondering the situation. Almost a year and a half had gone by since I had first crossed her path. She decided to forego the temptation to wallow in bitterness against God, and felt that He simply employed a special softening process on what she defined as her stony heart.

Suddenly the stillness of the predawn hour was broken by a powerful gust of wind. A still small voice whispered to Rimona, "Just as that sudden gust of wind changed the environment in an instant, so can the wind of my Spirit."

Rimona soon dismissed those words as issuing out of her own mind, but the experience was repeated twice more within a very short time. Still, Rimona attributed the thought to herself.

We had planned to meet at my apartment in the morning, before going to breakfast. Not being aware of her plan to leave so soon, and just before going out of the door, I was taken up by the brief and mundane task of sweeping the kitchen floor.

Rimona happened to walk in at that moment, and looking up at her, I was suddenly overwhelmed with a feeling of love—a pure, holy, and powerful love.

My response to that sudden change was to inform Rimona that God really loved her. I no sooner got those words out of my mouth when I heard that inner voice in my heart say, *"Yes, and I want you to be the channel of that love."*

At that moment I stopped what I was doing and walked over to Rimona. I mumbled something about the "holy hugs" we used to give our brothers and sisters in the fellowship in California, and then proceeded to gently embrace her, telling her the rest of what I had just heard.

Needless to say, she did not leave that morning as planned. Truly the winds of His Spirit had changed things in an instant!

## By the Jordan

We spent the Shabbat together by walking down to the Jordan River, sitting on its bank and looking up at the Golan Heights. We talked about different things while walking hand in hand.

Rimona left the following morning for Jerusalem with the taxi that delivered the newspapers to the kibbutz. When she stepped into the vehicle a song was playing on the radio. It was a song that spoke about letting things be, as we have no control over the future. This was the same song she heard on the bus on her sad departure after the first visit to the kibbutz, almost nine months earlier.

As the taxi descended down the winding road toward the Sea of Galilee, the clouds over the water formed into a figure of a man. And while the figure had slowly become misshapen, as the form of the clouds changed, the feet remained intact and hovered for a long time over the body of water. Her inner being was full of the wonderment of a mysterious, loving Heavenly Father.

*"What will happen next?"* she wondered. *"When will we meet again?"*

About a week or so later I had gone to work at my usual time of 5:00 a.m., but instead of slowly and calmly working my way into my day, it started with a great deal of pressure. Around 6:30 a.m., the phone rang and I was called over. It was not a good time to be called to the phone, but the person who shouted to me insisted that it was urgent. Since I was already quite irritated, I responded impatiently to whom I thought was a very hysterical woman.

It turned out that within a few days of Rimona's return to Jerusalem, God had taken away her job, her roommate left unexpectedly, and at the same time the year's contract for the apartment was coming to an end, and the landlord wanted to know whether she was going to renew it. Being unsure of what she was to do, she called me.

Feeling as though I was somehow supposed to solve her problems, I was rather short and without mincing words blurted, "What? Do you want me to marry you or something?"

Trying to make up for my sudden curt remark, my next response was very "spiritual." I told her to go to her believing friends and pray, and that I would do the same, and that we would "meet in the heavenlies."

This suggestion, especially the reference to the "meeting in the heavenlies," baffled Rimona. As a fairly new Believer she was under the impression that the veterans had it all together, yet even with that, she was somewhat unsettled at the suggestion and wondered if I was able to think in practical terms. However, she did pray with a friend, who happened to be a Catholic nun with a very Jewish name.

Sister Marie Goldstein had a Jewish father, but was not raised Jewish. During that prayer the Holy Spirit showed Rimona that she was to go to the kibbutz in twelve days time. In my prayer time with Gary, I felt that I was to invite Rimona to the kibbutz.

When I called within a few days, I informed her of what I had gotten in my spirit. She however, was determined not to disclose to me what she had heard until hearing from me, as she had been wondering if I would confirm her spiritual sensing.

At the end of that week I went to Jerusalem to help her move from her apartment and to put some of her belongings in storage. The following day we took a taxi to Tel Aviv, so I could meet her parents.

I was a little nervous, as we stood in front of the door waiting for it to open...

## Meeting the In-Laws

Rimona's father immediately started bombarding me

with questions. Knowing that I was a Gentile and a Christian, he asked me if I would convert.

I gave him the same answer that I did to the kibbutz Social Committee, namely that "I cannot lie in order to become Jewish. It is simply a contradiction in terms."

I gave this answer because a convert is required to promise to keep all Jewish (*Halachic*) law, as determined by the Rabbinate. As a Believer and a kibbutz member, I could not subject myself to all these rulings, and neither could I pretend to the religious authorities that I would.

The next set of questions had to do with my profession. When I told Rimona's father that I was a Special Education teacher, and that I had worked with multi handicapped children and helped train their parents, his countenance changed, and so did the tone of our conversation. He suddenly became very interested in what I had to say, because Rimona had a younger sister who had been retarded from an early childhood disease. She had died less than two years earlier at the age of twenty-one.

Mordechai now talked with me as if we had known each other for many years. As a matter of fact, this was the very first time he had ever shared his pain outside the immediate family circle. Toward the end of our visit he even pulled out a bottle of wine and some wine glasses, and blessed our relationship.

At that point we told him, and Rimona's mother (Zahava), that in one week's time she was moving to the kibbutz.

It was December 25, 1981 when I went to the intersection to pick up Rimona, exactly twelve days after she had prayed with the Catholic Sister. However, when the bus arrived, Rimona was not on it. I thought maybe she was coming on another bus, so I waited. About fifteen minutes later a big semi truck, coming from the counter direction, pulled up and here was Rimona climbing down with her two suitcases.

I was so surprised to see her come from the opposite direction and out of such a vehicle that I didn't even get out of the car to help her with the luggage. My response, was not, of course, untypical of what had transpired up to that point in our relationship.

## The Little Envelope

Back at the kibbutz, I helped Rimona settle into her apartment and introduced her to the Social Committee which was responsible for taking care of her needs.

The kibbutz members were buzzing about this new arrival, the one known as "Ephraim's girlfriend." This kind of response was typical of the kibbutz, all the more so because many had given up the hope that I would ever be paired off.

The following day, which was a Shabbat, Rimona came over before going to brunch in the communal dinning hall. She joined me in the living room where I was reading my Bible. At that point, the little envelope, which had been in my Bible for two years, dropped out onto my lap.

In the course of the time that had elapsed, I had forgotten all about it. But when it landed on my lap I picked it up, and without thinking too much, handed it to Rimona, saying nonchalantly, "Here, this is yours."

The tiny engagement ring, like Cinderella's slipper, fit her finger perfectly.

Later in the day, my niece, whom I hadn't seen since her arrival in the Land, came by to pay me a visit.

As it turned out, each Shabbat she had been trying to make her way to Gadot, but had not succeeded until that day. Julie was surprised to see me with this new friend, and even more so when she noticed the ring on Rimona's finger.

It didn't take her long to pronounce us "engaged."

## Seventeen

# A War and a Wedding

Julie told us that her parents, my sister and brother-in-law, would be coming to visit her in June, so we planned to have the wedding on the kibbutz during their visit.

June rolled around quickly, and it happened that one of the members' eighty-year-old-father, a Conservative Rabbi from Argentina, was going to be in the Land at the time (in those years he actually made his home in Switzerland).

The old Rabbi agreed to come and officiate at the wedding, something he hadn't done for more than ten years. That is, providing that I would write a note stating my Jewish ancestry.

We invited our friends, and Rimona's parents invited relatives and more friends. Her cousin, a member of the Egged bus cooperative, volunteered to be the driver who would bring the guests to the kibbutz for the wedding.

The kibbutz members were preparing for the big day and the reception, the latter to be attended only by our special guests, as was kibbutz custom. But things were destined to take a different turn, because a few days before our wedding, some northern communities were hit by Katyusha rockets sent from across the Lebanon border.

Julie's kibbutz was located right on that border. She and her parents, Phyllis and Mike, had been touring the area when the attack came. In fact, some rockets had landed not too far from them. Nonetheless, they were able to make it back to the kibbutz, but had to spend the night in the bomb shelter.

When the sixth of June 1982, came around, the day before the wedding, there was a peculiar quietness in the dinning hall. That morning, many of the women showed up without their husbands, and the high school children were in work clothes. They were preparing for assigned tasks in the various work places, as many of the men had been called up during the night.

Because of the proximity of our kibbutz to the battle zone, I suggested to one of the members that we postpone the wedding. He responded in no uncertain terms: *"We do not cancel life because of war!"*

Rimona and I left early that morning to go to a nearby religious town to buy a Ketuba (a traditional Jewish marriage contract). But the one place that advertised hand drawn Ketubas was closed.

From there we proceed to Julie's kibbutz to pick up the family and bring them down to ours. On the way the roads were lined with military vehicles. Things looked rather ominous, but we did not know that Israel was poised to go into Lebanon on a major offensive.

When we arrived at Kibbutz Yiftach, they were just closing up the gates and the residents were going down into the bomb shelters. Julie and her parents were standing at its door when we drove up.

They quickly grabbed their belongings and hurriedly got out. Within a few minutes the Israeli Army was to go into Lebanon.

As we were driving up, we saw smoke in the fields where a Katyusha rocket had fallen a few hours before.

When we finally arrived at home, we settled our guests in an adjoining apartment that belonged to my boss, who was still in Denmark with his wife's family.

Late that afternoon, as we were showing my family around the kibbutz, we could hear the guns of war and see the jets circling amidst the clouds and the billows of black smoke on the northern sky line.

As we rounded one of the children's houses (at that time the kibbutz children still had their own quarters), we noticed a young teenage girl sitting on a heap of rocks over the top of one of the bomb shelters. Her legs were folded up to her chest, her arms wrapped them in an embrace and her chin was resting in the fold of her knees, while her eyes were fixed on the northern horizon. She was the daughter of one of the kibbutzniks who was a reserve officer and was now in Lebanon. As we passed by, she didn't look up, nor did she seem to be even aware of us. She was completely engrossed in her thoughts.

That evening we all sat on the lawn, reminiscing, praying, talking about the situation in Lebanon and thinking about the big day that was ahead of us.

After breakfast the next morning we all decided to take a walk down to the Jordan River. The day was warming up quite rapidly, so the one mile walk was just enough to work up a little sweat.

When we arrived, Rimona decided that she wanted to take a dip, even though she wasn't dressed for it. Later we realized that unwittingly she had fulfilled the Jewish tradition of *mikveh* (immersion) for the bride before her wedding. This was another demonstration of the Lord's sovereignty over our lives.

When we returned to the kibbutz, we found that Rimona's parents had arrived, with her aunts and uncle. We thought they were coming with the other relatives on the bus. However, they informed us that the bus, along with the bus driver, had been inducted into army duty.

A few close friends started to arrive, but because of the call-up and the situation in the North, many just couldn't make it. We consigned ourselves to visiting with the guests who did arrive.

The ceremony was to take place outside, in the courtyard of the dinning hall, at around sunset.

Several hours before the wedding we went around with the kibbutz's official photographer for a series of pre-wedding photos.

## The Ketuba

Upon arriving back at the house, one of the kibbutz artists presented us with a beautiful Ketuba (since we were not able to obtain one). He had made it from photocopies of a Ketuba belonging to another kibbutz member who handed it to him for this very purpose. In fact, she was the one who came up with the idea of creating such a Ketuba. He had hand-colored it, making it a unique creation that only our loving Father could have managed for this special day.

The Ketuba came none too soon, as the old Rabbi had just arrived, having made his way from a kibbutz near Nahariya through the slow moving military traffic.

Soon we met in the little kitchen area of my apartment, almost in the exact spot where I had been standing, broom in hand, when I heard the inner voice speak the words of becoming a channel of God's love to Rimona. Now those words were being sealed by our signatures on the Ketuba, along with the Rabbi's signature and those of our two witnesses.

Rimona's wedding dress was another gift, one that had a story behind it similar to that of the engagement ring.

A couple of months before the wedding, Rimona's mother was approached by a friend who had in mind the prefect wedding gown that she had seen worn by another bride, and insisted that Rimona should borrow it. Much to Rimona's own surprise, the gown not only fit her perfectly, but its style was tailor made for her taste. The stage was set for the next and final episode—two single people meeting in a divine bond of the covenant.

As a bride and groom we walked together toward the dinning hall. When we rounded the corner, we briefly noticed a wonderful display of flower-decorated tables laden with food, and a raised platform that had been set up for the ceremony

A new announcement in the dinning room foyer, which covered the old one, told the members that since most of the wedding party could not attend due to the war, they were now invited to partake in the reception as well.

## Under the Huppa

The path to the Huppa was illumined by the setting sun that colored the sky, with the clouds and the hazy smoke that had filtered down from the war forming a mixture of glowing tones of a yellow and orange backdrop. The Huppa, which was made kibbutz-style, using an Israeli flag fastened on its four corners to pitchforks and held up by four men, beckoned to us. The Rabbi, and Rimona's parents, were already under it, awaiting our arrival.

Compared to other wedding ceremonies at the kibbutz, there seemed to be a different air about this one. I looked around at the familiar faces, mostly women, thinking to myself that I should have been with the men in Lebanon, but then I remembered the exhortation, "We don't cancel life because of war!"

Everyone was busy talking when suddenly, in one of the strongest baritone voices I have ever heard, the eighty-year-old Rabbi pierced the evening air by singing the words: *"Baruch atah Adoni..."* (Blessed are you Lord God...)

Chills went up my spine, and the hair on my arms literally stood on end. The crowd was silenced and every eye (dry and wet alike) was glued on the event.

Then came my turn to declare and affirm our relationship, by repeating after the Rabbi, "Taking a wife according to the custom of Moshe and Israel..."

Drinking the wine was followed by the customary

crushing of a glass underfoot by the groom (in memory of the destruction of the Temple). This final event always generates a loud cheer of *Mazal Tov!* (*Congratulations*) from the crowd, and it did in our case too.

As we stepped off the platform, a large group of five-year-olds surrounded us with song, dance, and flowers. They were Rimona's kindergarten children, those whom she was in charge of in her work place.

We then proceeded to carry out Kibbutz Gadot's tradition of breaking a clay pot together.

*"How symbolically appropriate!"* we both thought. Time seemed to stop, and we were suspended in an aqua aura of heavenly presence.

We were flooded with warm and lovely smiles from the faces of those around us. We were kissed, embraced and encouraged with blessings. The war and the sounds of death truly did give way to life that evening!

The reception began before we realized it, and the food was consumed before either Rimona or I had a chance to even take a whiff at the wonderful preparations of the kitchen crew. We did, however, get a small bite of our wedding cake. The many still photos and moving pictures that were taken then would tell the tale of June 7, 1982, and would allow us to see some of what had escaped our notice during this special occasion.

We ended the evening outside our apartment, sitting on the lawn with our friends, singing, praising and reminiscing the day. At one point the bride became very hungry, as beside the bite of the wedding cake she had not had anything to eat the whole day. One of our friends volunteered to go to the kibbutz kitchen and get her something to eat. However, since the kitchen door was already bolted up, the food that the friend procured for Rimona was obtained by an arduous effort of climbing through metal bars and sneaking into the pantry.

## The Honeymoon

Early the following day we set out for Jerusalem with Phyllis, Mike and Julie, in one of the kibbutz vehicles. We decided to stop on our way and have a little dip in the Sea of Galilee. As we traveled down the eastern shore we could not even see across, as the haze and smoke from the war had filled the basin of the valley.

We were the only souls on the road and on the beach. It was a little eerie, to say the least, but we enjoyed life as we frolicked in the water. As honeymooners, we continued our journey down to Jericho, where we had lunch in an Arab restaurant with a ceiling that looked like the top of a cherry or strawberry meringue pie. From there we made our way up to Jerusalem for a wedding reception and conferring of blessings on the newlyweds, put on by Rimona's congregation and friends.

Once again, we experienced a gathering marked by our Shepherd God's love toward us, as expressed by our spiritual family.

We had planned to stay in Jerusalem for a few days and take our guests around. However, the next day we heard on the news the names of the war casualties. One of the names was that of Shai from Kibbutz Gadot. He was the young photographer that had worked with me in the welding shop, and his funeral was to be held the following day.

Rimona and I cut short our honeymoon, and headed back up to the kibbutz to make it on time for the funeral.

We returned to a somber community.

However, the challenges of living life amidst the reality of tragedies were not new to the people of this kibbutz, as it was nearly demolished by the Syrians in the 1967 War. Now, once again, the members all walked as one behind a bereaved family. They quietly proceed to the graveyard located on a hill near the orange groves and cotton fields.

One could look down the Hula Valley from there and

see the Golan Heights and Mount Hermon, as well as the Lebanese border.

That day, another young nineteen-year-old found his way into the soil of Israel before his time.

Before he enlisted into the army, Shai had given me an enlarged black and white photo that he had taken of me welding an old wheel barrel. It is a memento that I still treasure.

Rimona and I decided that we should go immediately back to work. It seemed the only right thing to do as many were missing from the work force because of the war.

## Married Life

Married life seemed to quickly fall into routines of work, social activities, and most of all getting to know one another better, as we were learning that marriage is a process and not a one time happening.

We started discovering things about each other that were hidden treasures of blessings. A few other things seemed to be insurmountable problems. And we soon found that about the only thing we had in common was our faith.

Since then it has become apparent to us during our twenty-some years of marriage that this was the best and most important foundation that our lives together could possibly be built upon.

Nevertheless, there were many times when I thought that Rimona should be different from what she was. But thinking that I could change her was an illusion. The idea that I could play the potter and she would be the clay very quickly crashed in on me. I had to come to terms with the fact that I was no creator.

## My "Ezer K'negdo"

My Heavenly Father had to teach me that He created her to be my *"ezer k'negdo"* (Genesis 2:20). That is, someone who would stand in front of me like a mirror, and help me see myself for who I really was and am.

During one of the more intense arguments, our Savior and Preserver of the relationship had to set us down and simply instruct us that the way to unity was for the two of us to draw close to, and keep our eyes on Him.

We are still learning this lesson.

Later on in that first year we traveled to the United States to visit my family, since my parents had not yet met my bride. Additionally, because our wedding was performed by a Rabbi from the Conservative Movement, which doesn't have an official status in Israel, where only the Orthodox give official religious services, we had to have a civil wedding (something that can't be done in Israel). So off we went to the court house in Wisconsin and had a civil ceremony.

## A Four Year Long Saga

With our marriage officially recognized by the State of Israel, I could now accomplish my Aliya (official immigration to Israel), which amazingly did not take more than in a few hours in the offices of the Jewish Agency in New York, although I did have a great deal of the paper work taken care of by the Jewish Agency's representative in Milwaukee, Wisconsin before making the trip to New York.

Within two days of arriving in New York, we were back in the Land, with my official Aliya date being December 31, 1982.

All in all, the process of transplanting me took four years. Thus the dream that the Spirit gave me back in 1976, in which I saw myself entering a little outhouse surrounded by a cyclone fence with barbed wire around the top, going down four stories while losing my clothes and wallet, and coming back up and out, wearing some kind of a uniform with someone next to me, came to pass.

The four stories were the four years on the kibbutz,

which was surrounded by a cyclone fence with barbed wire. The loss of my clothes and wallet meant a change of identity, while the uniform was the kibbutz blue work clothes. The one standing next to me was of course my wife.

Upon our return, the kibbutz's Social Committee suggested another Ulpan (Hebrew language school) session for me, as this was one of my rights as a new immigrant. I was sent to one of the best schools in Israel, Ulpan Akiva in Netanya. It was there that my life took another one of those incredible turns, but not because I succeeded in learning the language.

Our wedding under the Huppa in Kibbutz Gadot, on June 7th 1982, the second day of the Lebanon War. The smoke in the background was rolling out of Lebanon as the sun was setting.

Rimona and her parents in front of
Ephraim and Rimona's kibbutz apartment.

Ephraim in the kibbutz welding shop.
Photo by Shai, from Kibbutz Gadot,
a young photographer who
gave his life in defense of the Land.

# Eighteen

# M'lo Ha-Goyim

We were in the final week of the Hebrew Ulpan program, and as part of our daily study routine I was given to read (in Hebrew) a section from the Torah.

The portion happened to be Genesis 48:8-20. As I got to the part about Israel pronouncing his blessing on the heads of Menashe and Ephraim, it was as if I heard him speaking it for the first time to his grandson, Ephraim: "And your seed will become *m'lo ha-goyim—the fullness of the nations.*"

I paused for an extra long moment. Revelation was shooting through me like fire. Everyone was looking, waiting for me to continue; the teacher even tried to help me along by reading the next few verses.

After class I went back to my room and grabbed my Green's Interlinear Hebrew–Greek Bible. I flung it open to the page of that Scripture and read it again, this time in English.

The question that came to mind as I read about the "fullness of the Gentiles" or "nations," was, *"Is this the same 'fullness of the Gentiles' that Paul spoke of in Romans 11?"*

The answer came bursting into my bones like a bomb, *"Yes, of course!"* And that answer almost knocked the wind out of me. I must have wept for an hour as this reality worked its way into my soul.

# Return to the Land

Being overwhelmed with my discovery, I was glad it was Friday and time to go home to the kibbutz.

On the bus I sat back in my seat and opened my Bible to Romans 11:25-29, where I read more than a dozen times: "For I do not desire, brethren, that you should be ignorant of this mystery, lest you should be wise in your own opinion, that blindness in part has happened to Israel until the fullness of the nations come in. And so all Israel will be saved, as it is written: 'The Deliverer will come out of Zion, and He will turn away ungodliness from Jacob; for this is My covenant with them, when I take away their sins.' Concerning the gospel they are enemies for your sake, but concerning the election they are beloved for the sake of the fathers. For the gifts and the calling of God are irrevocable" (NKJV).

As the bus made its way down the winding road into Tiberius, my desire to share my news with someone else compelled me. I got off the bus near the home of the brothers who had moved from Rosh Pina, and were now residing in the town on the shores of the Sea of Galilee.

Both Reuven and Benjamin were home, and I immediately began to share with them these Scriptures. Although they were very cordial, I sensed their cautious skepticism, and then heard them say something about "British Israelism." However, since I was in a hurry to catch the last bus to the kibbutz before Shabbat, I didn't have time to discuss the issue any further.

With the new revelation that was now burning inside me, I couldn't wait to share my news with Rimona, who only added more fuel to my fire.

She too was of the opinion that the verse spoke of the "Gentile Believers." She had felt this ever since she first began to read the Word when she came to faith.

At one point before we met, she had asked the wife of a pastor of an American congregation in Jerusalem about this idea, and she was told that "some people do believe that."

The idea made sense to Rimona because she had grown up in Israel and had learned history and Tanach (Old Testament) in school. She knew of the place of these lost ones in Jewish lore, and of the Jewish expectation that one day, they would be restored to the Nation. She even reminded me that we had actually discussed the topic a few times during our sporadic meetings in Jerusalem, long before we were married.

## Always on My Mind

About this time, my former boss came back to the kibbutz and had taken over the welding branch again, and I was assigned to the dinning hall. However, I was so consumed by the revelation that I couldn't eat, even though working ten hours a day and being around food in my current job.

After work I spent most of my nights studying and searching out the Scriptures, which now seemed to be completely different from what I had known them to be in the past.

In addition, at the time I was reading a book called *The Zionist Ideal*, which added to my excitement and reinforced the idea of the "return to the Land." These early Zionist philosophers' and visionaries' writings confirmed what I was seeing from the pages of the prophets. The combination of these two sources of inspiration held me in a state of exhilaration which energized and stimulated me both intellectually and emotionally.

After forty days of working, studying, and not eating, my wife was getting concerned. She thought that perhaps her new husband would be "raptured," in a form of a thin vapor, into heaven.

One day I woke up feeling a strong urge to find someone among the Believers who could confirm this notion of the "Two Houses of Israel." Three persons came to my mind, all of whom were from Jerusalem.

## Seeking Confirmation

In my zeal I took a day off work and set out to look for them, even though I had not made prior arrangements.

The first person that I wanted to talk to was my old prayer partner, who was now the chairman of the International Christian Embassy in Jerusalem.

Johann was in his office when I arrived. Right away I started to fly through the Scriptures, explaining to him how I saw the mystery of Romans 11.

He rolled his chair away from the desk, leaned back, crossed his arms and listened intently. After about a half an hour of watching me swing from the chandeliers he said in a very soft melodic South African accent: "You prophets are all alike, crazy!" and then added: "Maybe you should talk with Jan Willem."

He was actually the second person I had in mind to talk to. So I walked across the hall to Jan Willem's office, and he too happened to be there.

With only a few minutes to spare, he listened to the notions that came sputtering out of my mouth—at a pace that defied a listener's ability to comprehend.

Still, his comments were encouraging. Jan Willem agreed that most likely there were those in the Church who were descendants of the lost Israelites.

After that I took a bus to Motza, which is just outside of Jerusalem, to see the third person on my mental list. David Biven was at home when I arrived, so I repeated for the third time my new understanding of the verses I had found in the Scriptures.

David told me that he didn't really comprehend this topic, but knew of someone in the States who was teaching something much like what I was describing. He also said that they were coming for the Feast of Tabernacles in the Fall, and that he would introduce me to them.

I went back to the kibbutz relieved that I wasn't totally crazy, and that which I had understood was quite possibly true.

## From the Galilee to Judea

Working in the dining hall was probably the best place for me, as I was kept busy serving the entire kibbutz populace. With lots of faces and constant activity I was distracted from my obsession.

By this time Rimona had also become a member of the kibbutz, as she only had one year of candidacy to qualify for membership. She enjoyed working in the children's house with the five and six year olds, but was not always agreeable to the kibbutz environment and the dynamics produced by a society of this type.

During the summer of 1983 I was becoming more and more restless. Life on the kibbutz seemed to be coming to an end. I was burning with the desire to go out and spread the message about the "other house" of Israel.

Rimona, perhaps for other reasons, was also ready to leave. In addition, I was toying with the idea of writing a book. So we started praying about leaving. Where to go and how to support ourselves were two major concerns, and we were in the dark as to solutions. Life on the kibbutz was very secure, and I had often thought that this way of life would also be great for Believers.

In spite of our unresolved problems, we did eventually approach the Social Committee with the idea of leaving and pursuing our other aspirations.

They graciously offered us a year's sabbatical, during which we could try to satisfy our yearnings. But we felt that if our God were calling us into a ministry, we would have to make the break and sever the relationship for good, which for me, after five years of being in this new family, was not an easy decision.

The Lord helped me along through a dream, in which

# Return to the Land

I saw what looked like kibbutz buildings, with a rose garden, and five very withered rose bushes. Milling around its edges were people who resembled some of the kibbutz members. The interpretation came almost as soon as I woke up.

## Shechem

The rose bushes were the five Believers who were living on the kibbutz. Apparently the kibbutz was not conducive to the spiritual growth of Believers.

Another confirmation came after we asked the Lord where we were to go. One morning, as I was reading 2 Chronicles, some words stood out to me like a red fire engine: "Then Rehoboam went to Shechem, for all Israel had come to Shechem to make him king" (10:1).

I was immediately filled with a strong sense that we were to go to Shechem, but kept it to myself. However, later that day, Rimona approached me with a Scripture that had stood out to her while reading 2 Kings: "Then Rehoboam went to Shechem, for all Israel had come to Shechem to make him king" (12:1).

I was absolutely speechless!

We didn't need any more witnesses or confirmations, yet there was a major problem with the idea.

Shechem was a large Arab city, a Muslim stronghold having no Jewish residents at all. Nevertheless, we were willing to pitch a tent somewhere in the area if that was where we were to go.

At the time we had not considered the idea of a settlement in the nearby area, or anywhere for that matter.

Although we had to shelve the idea of moving to Shechem or its prophetic environs, we still felt the parallel Scriptures that had stood out to us confirmed that leaving the kibbutz was the order of the day.

In the meantime, Rimona had confided in a friend from Jerusalem that we were planning to move out of

Gadot. It just happened that this friend had purchased an apartment in a new area outside Jerusalem, on the edge of the Judean desert, and was looking for tenants. With this in mind, she asked us if we would be interested in renting it from her.

It occurred to us that this might be a launching pad for our new undertaking.

## Launching Out

The kibbutz was very efficient when it came to business transactions, so closing our accounts and receiving what was comparable to severance pay was not a problem. The amount we received seemed sufficient for about six months of living expenses, and with that we proceeded with our ideas and vision.

Rimona left the kibbutz a day before I did, to go and get things ready at our new residence. I stayed back to pack our things in the kibbutz van with the help of a friend. The following day, when I arrived at the apartment, I was welcomed by an angry and despondent wife. In spite of solemn promises, the apartment was not at all ready for occupants; there was no electricity, no gas, a lot of dust and dirt without any cleaning materials, and no offer of help from our friend-cum-landlady, who left us to cope with the situation on our own. Having no other alternative, we unloaded our belongings and stacked them all into one of the bedrooms.

As we were unpacking the van, the bright sky was suddenly covered with thousands of storks circling above the buildings. My kibbutz friend, who was helping me, looked up and said to us: "You two are going to have lots of children."

We equated his prediction with a ministry of birthing in many others the revelation-understanding of the whole commonwealth of Israel.

## Tent Life?

Our new location and housing situation were almost as good as living in a tent. Thankfully, a young couple living next door ran an electric cord over, and we had a lamp for the evening light. Days were spent making the apartment livable, especially the floors, which we polished by hand.

Rimona's parents gave us a single bed with a mattress and a box spring. I converted the bed frame into a closet, while laying the other two parts side by side on the floor, and covering them with a large double foam mattress that we had from the kibbutz.

Slowly we got the apartment into shape, and within two weeks we had electricity and gas. So we continued our second year of marriage, almost in the exact state that I saw us in the dream; walking out of an open gate into a blue sky, with a fence and barbed wire off to the side, which this Judean Desert settlement was also surrounded with.

We left the kibbutz in the beginning of August 1983, and by September, I started what I thought was going to be a book.

I kept busy researching and typing out the Scriptures that were relevant to the revelation of the "Two Houses," but without a computer it was a very tedious task. However, what became quite apparent, almost from the start, was that most of the Scriptures that I had found started with the words, "Thus says the Lord..."

## Tabernacles

When the Feast of Tabernacles rolled around, I called David Bivin to see if that couple he had told me about was still coming to the Land. He reassured me that they were, and we made a date to meet Angus and Batya Wootten at the International Convention Center in Jerusalem.

On the day we met there were probably no other people on the face of the earth more excited than the four of us. In the course of their stay we saw them a few more times, including one time at our home in Maale Adumim, at which time David and his wife came too.

These were the most encouraging meetings that we could have ever had. Angus and Batya had been tackling the "Two House" issue for a couple of years, so they were confirming everything that we knew up that point, as well as sharing more from their own understanding.

They also verified our suspicions that there were not many who understood this truth, and even fewer who supported such a revolutionary revelation.

When Angus and Batya left, I resumed working on the task that was before me. I knew that I had about five more months to accomplish it, so I continued researching, "Thus says the Lord."

# Return to the Land

## Nineteen

# The Excursion

Toward the end of December 1983, on a Friday, while sitting in a little cubbyhole of a buffet-restaurant in Jerusalem, we happened to catch a glimpse of an acquaintance passing by on the street.

Grant was a one-armed newspaper reporter who sometimes showed up at our fellowship meetings in Jerusalem, sharing with us about the woes of the Christians in war-torn Lebanon. I jumped off my stool and ran out to greet him and to find out what he was up to. This quick chance encounter started one of the most exciting episodes of our new life outside the kibbutz.

Grant told us about his work with the Christians in Southern Lebanon. He elaborated a little on the genocide that was fully under way, with the world ignoring the crimes committed by the Muslims, who wiped out entire Christian villages by applying the worst types of cruelties. He then mentioned that he, along with some others, were planning to leave the next day to go to a besieged Christ-ian village in the Shouff Mountains east of Beirut, called Deir el Kamar. They wanted to take food and clothing to the villagers and to spend Christmas with them.

Before we parted, he mentioned that we would be welcome to join them. Not thinking too much about the complications involved, or about how hazardous this could be, we said, "Yes."

With a quick handshake and with parting words of instructions to be at his house in Metula near the "Good Fence" the following morning, he was off, adding that one of the assistant pastors of our congregation was planning to drive there and could also take us.

Arriving in Metula the following Shabbat morning, with just a handbag equipped for a one night visit, we were not quite sure what to expect. Grant, his wife, and quite a few others, were huddled together and praying intensely in the small, dimly lit makeshift house.

Grant had been working with another individual, Bruce, who was also involved with the Christian Lebanese. The two of them were trying to coordinate the trip. They were in intense prayer because the permit that the Israeli Army commander was supposed to grant to the convoy had not yet been given. It had been promised in no uncertain terms days before, but now, just before take off time, the Israeli guards by the Good Fence had not received any orders to let such a convoy go through.

We continued waiting for an hour or so, praying and believing that the door would eventually open. Grant kept talking on the telephone and taking trips to the fence, but to no avail. At one point, however, he gave marching orders. So we climbed into the vehicles and proceeded toward the Fence. The two of us went with some people from our congregation in an old VW van.

## The Shouff Mountain Convoy

The convoy consisted of eight vehicles and approximately thirty people. One vehicle was from Bethlehem, with a couple of very old and dear Christian Arab saints who looked much like nuns. They had with them a few young men with musical instruments and drums. Their driver happened to be a Muslim. There were also several journalists who were going to cover the event. Another car had a couple with their three small children. This family lived in this northernmost village of Metula, but worked at the Christian radio station in Southern Lebanon. It was quite an assortment of individuals.

When we arrived at the fence, still without a permit, there were only a couple of soldiers there. Grant, Bruce, and a few of the others got out, exchanged words with the young men, and within a few minutes the gates were opened!

Bruce, in the first car, followed by the family (which had a regular pass), went right through. I was wondering who might be stopped, and at which point along the way. But when the vehicle from Bethlehem, with a non-Israeli license plate and with Arabs in it, was allowed to continue, it was becoming clear that we were traveling on a God-paved road of miracles.

We continued on our way without any problem; every now and then coming across Israeli soldiers who always let us proceed after a few short exchanges.

After a time, the road became rough with many potholes, but as we were leaving the Galilee behind us, the loveliness of the higher elevations of the rugged terrain decorated by spots of snow made up for the physical discomfort.

After less than two hours we stopped in the town of Jezzin, where the beauty of the South Mediterranean, both natural and man-made, that Lebanon used to be so famous for, could still be detected. We refueled and paused to take a breath of fresh air. The crisp, clear air and the sights around us were very refreshing after traveling in that old fume-filled vehicle.

Within another hour or so we were almost out of the territory of Israel's military control. The roads were getting rougher, and more dangerous, and so was the local populous. We were approaching an area of Lebanon that was controlled by the Druze.

Before we got to that point, we stopped to remove the Israeli license plates from the vehicles, and to wait for the previously-arranged-for group of Druze notables, who had agreed to accompany our convoy and to protect us from hostile encounters.

As we continued on our way we realized why we needed their protection. Alongside the road there were many young children (about twelve years of age), dressed in military uniform with automatic weapons in their hands! No doubt, if it were not for our local guards we would have been running the gauntlet, and who knows what the results might have been!

The sun was starting to go down, and we had not arrived at our destination. We were told that the last leg of our journey would take us through the most dangerous area of all, a real "no-man's land."

With prayers in our hearts and on our lips (not that we had stopped praying at any other point in the journey), we were now being carried on angels' wings all the way to Deir el Kamar. And did we have a surprise awaiting us!

No sooner did we approach the entry road to this mountainous village, when we noticed, by way of our head lights, on each side of the narrow road a military formation consisting of the local militia. Popping out of the barrels of the M-16's and AK47's, which they held in front of them, were red and white carnations! This was but a prelude to what awaited our mission of goodwill and encouragement.

## A Truly Giving People

By the time we arrived at the village night had fully set in. It was ten o'clock and Christmas Eve. The main square was decorated with traditional trinkets but no lights, and the square itself was packed with people of every age. Mothers were holding babies in their arms, and everyone was pressing around the vehicles, cheering and waving.

Tears rolled down my cheeks as we opened the doors and met loving arms reaching out for us. We were all embracing and kissing total strangers with tears of joy.

An honorary and emotion-filled reception was waiting for us in the town hall, with the mayor and other dignitaries. We were welcomed with warm drinks and snacks, and each of us was handed a rose and sprig of cedar, and then we were assigned families that would host us for the night.

Next came the highlight of the visit, a Christmas Eve service at the local Maronite church building (most Lebanese Christians belong to that branch of the Catholic Church). The service was special, with music played by our band, testimonies, and the message of salvation and deliverance in the Name of Messiah Yeshua.

It was around midnight by the time we filed into the large, stark, and foreboding church building. However, in a short time it turned into a cheerful place, with words of hope being spoken and sung.

The family with their three children stood up and told why they had wanted to be there. Grant gave a message of salvation and we all sang together. One of the elderly saints from Bethlehem did all the translating, and of course was able to talk to the people directly and to minister to them.

Many responded to the call of God that night, while two of the young women from our fellowship, along with some others, volunteered to stay on in Deir el Kamar and disciple the newcomers to the Kingdom.

We were assigned to a lovely and hospitable family who only spoke Arabic and French, yet we managed to communicate in love, and to encourage them to walk with their Messiah in those very trying times.

What baffled us then (and to this very day), was how these people who had been under siege for months, managed to find so much delicious food (some canned) with which to feed us, while we supposedly had come to meet their needs!

The next morning we were able to admire the beauty of the village with its old, stylized graceful buildings and homes and surroundings. And then, another church service awaited us.

Our time was spent giving glory to God and trying to inspire our new friends to turn to a much greater Friend who longed for their friendship.

During both services the church was filled to over-flowing, especially during the second one. The pews were removed to make more room for everyone, for many refugees from other villages that had been overrun by the Muslims also attended this time.

After a short lunch it was time to say goodbye, as we had a long and arduous journey ahead of us if we were to make it to Israel by that evening. Being aware that the life of some of those whom we were hugging could be snuffed by their enemies in a very short time lent this goodbye an added dimension of sadness.

## Back to Israel

Starting our journey in daylight, and going over areas that we had already passed the day before set more confidence in our hearts.

The thought of traveling for so many long hours in a fume filled van was too much for Rimona. Therefore she asked if there would be room for her in any of the other vehicles, and she was invited to ride with the family from the radio station.

The journey home was uneventful, until we reached the Israeli border. This time there were more than a few soldiers waiting by the gate, and our convoy was held up.

We decided that the car with the family that had the pass to go into Lebanon would lead the way. They crossed into Israel without any problem, Rimona with them.

But the rest of us were detained with many questions being raised. The soldiers wanted to know if there were any Israelis among us, and someone pointed at me. Fortunately, I quickly hushed him and took out my American passport.

What a relief! Israeli citizens could get in big trouble for going to Lebanon. And the only one with a solely Israeli passport was Rimona, who was by then well out of harm's way!

After going through the gate and back into Israel, the family and Rimona waited on the other side to see what would become of us.

At one point during our questioning I was able to cross over and tell Rimona what had happened. And since my (American) passport was now being held, I was forced to return to the other side, while Rimona was invited to spend the night with the family she had ridden with.

We were told that our passports would be returned to us the following day, but we had no idea whether we would be allowed to go back into Israel.

Grant proceeded to lead our convoy back to a nearby village, where he had a believing friend. True to Lebanese hospitality, our now reduced crew of about twenty was given sleeping space on the floor, and something to eat the following morning.

Back at the border crossing the following day, we were processed out by the soldiers, some of whom, especially the girls, were looking at us as if we had just landed from outer space.

My feelings were not dissimilar to that impression, for I knew beyond a shadow of a doubt that I had just come back to earth from an experience that may as well have taken place on another planet.

## The Town Square at Deir el Kamar

## Twenty

# From House to House

After our incredible trip to Lebanon, it was back to abstracting, assembling, and placing the pieces of the puzzle, made up of Scripture verses, into what was becoming a readable text. I continued to be amazed every day at how many Scriptures portrayed this revelation; not only from the Old Testament, but now I was also beginning to understand why Yeshua said: "I have only come to the lost sheep of the house of Israel," and what He meant by, "another flock have I."

It was hard for me to understand why others could not see this very thing in the Scriptures, as the whole Bible seemed to be permeated with this truth.

When I finished the work, I photocopied the manuscript, bound it in spiral pamphlets, and excitedly sent or personally placed it into the hands of those whom I thought might help finance its publication.

To my sinking dismay, it was as if I had handed them Limburger cheese! I mourned for days. Our money was dwindling and our hoped for launching into ministry with this message was not going as well as anticipated.

## On to the Mount of Olives

Our time in the Judean Desert apartment was also coming to an end, as we could not afford to pay rent beyond the original seven months, and our landlords were not willing to grant us even one extra day.

In those days we felt that our circumstances were actually a test of our faith in the course of getting the ministry underway, so looking for jobs did not seem to be an option at that point.

While in prayer one morning, I felt that we were to move up to a large communal house on the Mount of Olives. A couple in our fellowship in Jerusalem lived there, taking care of the place for a ministry out of Norway. It was in their van that we had ridden through Lebanon.

For a number of years the Norwegians had an evangelistic outreach to the Arabs who lived in the area, but they were no longer living in Israel. Still, they had an extended vision for the building, and for the activities that they believed were to take place in it.

One thing stood in the way of my idea: I knew Rimona would be absolutely opposed to the scheme. She felt the couple that was heading this ministry was not totally credible, and she was not the only one who thought that. Others in our congregation had the same impression.

We were familiar with the huge and sterile Arab owned house that had an institutional feel about it, as we had participated in various functions that had taken place there. When I stated my thoughts about moving there to Rimona, she was not enthusiastic, to put it mildly. Our little nest had been built with sweat (and tears), and had been so short lived!

Rimona's apprehensions, together with the prospect of moving to a hostile Arab neighborhood, were enough to make the idea abhorrent to her. Having no other recourse, I put out a fleece: "If this is of You, Abba, show her that this is what we are to do." Then I had yet another dream: I saw the two of us walking out the door of our apartment and leaving all our belongings behind.

The time for the move was upon us, and one morning Rimona said that, while praying she was impressed by the words: "Go up to the mountain, to the House of the Lord."

That was all that I needed. I was willing to leave everything behind and take only the bare minimum of our belongings, and head up toward Jerusalem to the Mount of Olives.

The residents of the "Big House" were glad to hear that we were joining them, but Rimona would not agree to leaving all of our possessions behind. So we took our belongings with us. The house was certainly big enough to absorb every item.

Just before we made our moving arrangements, we started hearing that the believing community in Jerusalem (including our own congregation) was very displeased with the house residents and their activities.

They were labeled as false prophets and apostles who were allegedly spreading unsound doctrines. So, not only were we moving into a very precarious situation, we too were immediately under suspicion, especially by those who have heard us share about the Two Houses.

Nevertheless, we made our move and settled into one of the rooms that had a wonderful view westward, overlooking Jerusalem. From the roof there was an incredible panoramic sight of the Judean Desert, the Mount of Olives, Arab villages, and the Hill of Evil Counsel (where the U.N. headquarters is situated). We spent many hours in prayer up on the roof. There were times when we would get up at 2:00 or 3:00 in the morning and pray and praise until breakfast. We also had Bible studies and prayer meetings there. And someone had a vision of aerials sticking up out of the roof of the house. It was interpreted to mean that the house would become an international center for prayer and intercession, something that actually did materialize years later.

The two month long period that we stayed in the house had its ups and downs. For example, when on my way home one day, as I was strolling through the Old City of Jerusalem, my wallet was snatched from my back pocket.

Just a few minutes before the incident I heard the

inner voice say to me to remove my wallet and to place it in my satchel. However, I did not heed the directive, and immediately afterward I heard that same voice speaking to me again: "In the future, you are going to have to learn to listen, it could be a matter of life and death."

After reporting the incident to the Police, I proceeded back to the Mount of Olives. Exiting the Lions' Gate (also called St. Stephen Gate), I noticed that the street was cluttered with garbage, and in all the rubble I spotted a ball of paper. I took about three paces past it when I had an urge to go back and pick it up.

Having just learned a listening lesson, I did not hesitate this time. As I unfolded the crumpled piece of paper, it was, to my amazement, a torn-out page of an English Bible. A closer look showed it to be Ezekiel chapter two. As I walked and read, the Word of my God was ministering to my heart. My inner being was leaping and jumping with joy and praises.

It wasn't very long before the man who headed the ministry in the house proclaimed himself head apostle of Jerusalem. He believed that one day, all the pastors, who by now were very wary of him, would have to submit to his authority.

Rimona's suspicions turned out to be correct, and ultimately we were asked by the elders of our congregation to "flee the place." In fact, they gave us an ultimatum to leave that house or be dis-fellowshipped.

## Time to Move On

We had seen enough of this self-proclaimed, "chief apostle of Jerusalem," and we knew that our time at the "Big House" (as it was commonly called) was up. Our daily Scripture reading had also confirmed to us that this was the way we were to go.

At the time there was another couple who had been there for a short time, with whom we had become quite close. We decided that we would move out together. The day for the move approached, and we really didn't have a place to go to, and neither did our friends.

That very morning, to our total stunned surprise, a little yellow vehicle drove up to the entrance of the mansion, and an equally yellow-haired lady got out of it. She had been attending our congregation and knew of our predicament. "I came to take you home," she said determinedly, as she stepped out of her car.

"But there is another couple here with us, what about them?" we dared challenge.

"Bring them too," was the prompt answer.

It didn't take us very long to pack up our things, as we only took enough for our very basic needs. Besides, the "apostle" told us that we would not be able to take any of our other belongings from the house as, according to him, we had given it all to the community and to his ministry when we agreed to live there.

The rent for the house had not been paid for months and the owner was threatening to oust all the tenants. With all this (and more) going on, we felt that our belongings had been defiled and that we were to leave them all there, only to find out later that they were used as collateral for the unpaid rent.

The three months that were spent in that house, and in that peculiar situation, were not all bad. The Father was teaching us that He is sovereign over all our matters and that even though we may plan our way, He directs the path (reference Proverbs 16:9). And He does so with endless faithfulness.

## Homeless

Homeless but not hopeless, we were carried on the wings of the little yellow car. Along with our friends Bruce and Margaret we arrived now at the suburb of Gilo, which was where Rimona had lived when we first met.

# Return to the Land

The next couple of weeks were taken up by helping this friend, with whom we were now staying, move out of her apartment to a home in the very quaint Jerusalem neighborhood of Malcha, or Manachat. The backyard of her new home faced open countryside. Quite often we would spot small herds of deer and gazelles and other animals.

It seemed quite obvious that I would have to start looking for work. Having been a special education teacher in the United States, the most logical place to look for a job was the Ministry (Department) of Education.

My interviewer was very excited at the prospect of my joining the education establishment, in spite of my very weak Hebrew, as the needs seemed to be great. He even commented that I had nothing to worry about, since they would find me children to work with that could handle my level of Hebrew.

His words filled me with confidence that there was a job lined up for me. However, since I had not heard back from the Education Department after that initial interview, I decided to go back there.

This time, to my surprise, a hard and stony-faced individual, who put me off as though I had committed some indecent act, met me. He told me bluntly that there was nothing for me. I surmised that they must have found out that I was not Jewish, as the difference in attitude was very striking. I left the place in shock, addressing my Master with, "What now?"

Prayer was in order when I arrived back at the house. Our hostess happened to know someone who was volunteering in an institution for severally mentally and physically handicapped children in a beautiful Jerusalem neighborhood called Ein Kerem (Spring of the Vineyard, traditionally the birthplace of John the Baptist). She suggested that perhaps there would be some work, paid or otherwise, for me in that place, and so her friend, Robert, came to see us.

## A Local "Mother Teresa"

Robert was very enthusiastic about his work at the Catholic institute of St. Vincent and about his associations with the other volunteers, most of whom were Believers and lived on the premises.

Our friend took me to the institution that was run by French and Italian nuns. Aside from the volunteer staff there were also a number of paid Arab workers. The large building complex was surrounded by beautiful scenery of the Judean hills and boasted its own lovely gardens and olive groves that formed a miniature Garden of Eden, interspersed by a few statues. But the greatest treat in this paradise was meeting the founder, Sister Barnes.

Eighty-year-old Sister Barnes, stooped and wrinkled, had the most striking facial expression, with indelible etchings of wisdom, kindness, and compassion. She had led a life of devotion, dedication, and heroism. At risk to her own life she had hidden Jews from the Nazis during the Second World War in her native Italy. Now she was serving neglected and abandoned children that both families and society had cast out.

St. Vincent was home to Arab as well as Jewish children, not a few of whom were just left there and forgotten. Sister Barnes had been acknowledged for her work by the City of Jerusalem, and had received from then Mayor Teddy Kollek, who was her personal friend, the highest Jerusalem award. She was even made an honorary citizen of the city. In her own humble and cheerful way she was our local "Mother Teresa."

This elderly lady escorted me through the institution, going up and down stairs as if her eighty years did not faze her. The children I saw there ranged from the most severe, to low-level Down Syndrome and autistic, whose ages varied from infancy to adolescence. My heart was immediately drawn to them.

After the tour we talked about the possibilities of running a special program for the children, after school hours, since most of them were participating in a school run by the Ministry of Education that was housed in the institution.

Since we were now approaching the summer vacation, a three-week, full day special summer activity plan was lined up for them. I was to run it together with our friends, Bruce and Margaret, who were themselves first-rate professionals in the areas of care and welfare.

Mother Barnes wanted to use my expertise and perhaps implement an idea after the end of the school vacation, which she had tucked away in the back of her mind. She asked if my wife would come and work too. I was not able to give an answer at that moment, as in the past Rimona had found it difficult even visiting these types of places (where her own sister had been living for some years before her death).

I returned the following day, with Rimona, Bruce and Margaret. The four of us were interviewed and shown the place as well as the volunteer living quarters. We were all very moved as we went through the children's living area; even Rimona received a healing from her fears. We knew that this was what God was leading us into at that stage. We couldn't help associating the place and our experience with John the Baptist's words, "He must increase but I must decrease" (John 3:30, NKJV).

Within days we were fully enrolled in the work. We were given room and board and a small monthly stipend. The special program that was formulated by the heart of love of Sister Barnes was to create a family-like unit for some of the higher-level children, with a couple that could communicate with them in Hebrew (as the volunteers and the nuns did not speak the language).

Rimona and I were assigned eight children, four Down syndrome girls, two quadriplegic boys, another boy with multiple disabilities, and a cute, petit eight-year-old deaf girl who looked very normal but had severe behavioral problems.

Our assigned living quarters were in one of the back gardens and faced a lovely olive grove, which kept us reminded daily of the vision of the restoration of the family of Jacob. We had one bedroom with an adjoining bathroom. We named our new home, "The Cave."

## Our New Family

On our first morning on the job we were to wake the children, bathe, dress, and feed them and get them off to school. But because of the change that had taken place in their rooms, caretakers, and routines, the children, needed to test their (our) boundaries.

First to greet us was a certain odor that signified trouble. The petit eight-year-old girl, who had to be caged in an enclosed crib for the night because of her problematic and potentially disastrous behavior, had taken revenge.

She was the one responsible for the odor which emanated from every part of the room that was within reach of her little fingers. This was normal morning procedure for her.

Two of the Down Syndrome girls also needed an urgent change of clothes. The boys, on the other hand, thought it was funny and watched us as we waded through the task of clean up. The more mobile ones refused to cooperate, and at the same time we had to learn how to feed the quadriplegics, each of whom had a somewhat different way of taking in food.

Eventually we did get them off to school that day, albeit a little late and still somewhat smelly. We spent the rest of the morning cleaning, organizing the room and preparing to receive our new little family after school.

The days and weeks went by, and with God's help, we began to see changes in their behavior as they responded to love, rewards and occasionally a firm hand.

Within a short time we truly felt like a family, just as Sister Barnes had envisioned. Behavioral problems were still evident, but we knew that we were doing what Abba had meant for us to do. We also sensed that our experience with the retarded children was somehow parallel to the way the Shepherd/Parent of Israel was viewing His people. Evidently our spiritual condition is comparable to that of these helpless, dependant and handicapped children!

It was indeed a joy and a delight to discover the variety of personalities veiled behind institutional behaviors and exteriors; it was good to see the previously untapped potential of many of the children blossom forth.

Ofer was a six-year-old quadriplegic who had lived at home most of his life. Some time before we arrived, he was institutionalized, as his parents moved to Africa and believed that it would be too much for him to make the move. He understood only Hebrew and was now thrust into a world which seemed very strange and unfamiliar to him (and no doubt very frightening too).

He was assigned to our family group, and because we were speaking Hebrew, it was possible to communicate with him. Although he couldn't talk, his bright blue-gray eyes would lighten up whenever he was addressed. One day Rimona came up with an idea of conversing with him. She suggested that he look down at his right hand to signal "yes," and down at his left for a "no." When she realized that he understood her proposition, Rimona began to draw out information from him about his home life. We were both amazed how intelligent this little guy really was, while no one else in the institution, or even in the school, seemed to be aware of that fact.

Through an uncle we contacted his parents for pictures and tapes, which soon arrived. Ofer, with tears streaming down his little cheeks, would listen over and over to the voices of his parents and siblings, and for hours would gaze longingly at their photos, while we would cry right along with him. It was heart breaking to see this boy having to be away from his natural family, so we began to plead with them, as we passed on information about his emotional condition. Before we ourselves left, his parents, who were actually just as attached to him, came to take him home. We will never forget that day and the joy that the little boy exuded when he saw his mom come through the door.

Linda was the little girl who greeted us with the above-described savory scene. She was an Arab from Bethlehem who had been institutionalized for most of her life, and seemed extremely disturbed, yet was very capable, and when not displaying mischievous behavior, was made to help the staff. It took many months of tenacious love and discipline before trust began to penetrate her little heart. She, like Ofer, seemed quite normal inside, but because of her environmental handicaps that fact seemed to have escaped the notice of those who had been supervising her.

However, when we began to suspect that her hearing loss was more severe than thought, the sisters agreed to have her tested.

The results came back as we expected; she had almost no hearing at all. By that time her behavior had changed so much that it was decided to send her to a normal institution for the deaf in her hometown of Bethlehem. Two of the Down Syndrome girls had advanced so much during this period that they too were moved to a higher-level boarding school.

The ten months we spent at St. Vincent were an eye-opening time for us. While there, the Almighty blessed us with the good news that Rimona was pregnant, which immediately put us back on the path of seeking the Lord for our future, as we could no longer stay in our present circumstances.

*Above)* St. Vincent, Catholic Institution for
multi-handicapped children
Ein Karem, Jerusalem 1983-1984
*Below)* Ephraim and Rimona with their new little
family.

## Twenty-One

# Winds of Change

The news of Rimona's pregnancy rekindled a discussion we often had over the years about how and where we wanted our children to be born. Being blessed in this way, we now had to seek the Father for direction. Giving birth under the conditions that prevailed at the time in the maternity wards of Israel's hospitals was something Rimona was rather apprehensive about.

Once the news got out to family and friends, the prayers of many for this wayward couple that was now expecting their first child began their upward ascent.

A letter soon arrived from Wisconsin from my oldest sister, Phyllis, who said my brother's farmhouse was available for us to live in. That is, as long as it didn't sell. This seemed to be the answer we were seeking. In addition, on the neighboring farm, about one quarter of a mile away (less than one kilometer), there lived a believing midwife who was part of the fellowship that my sister and brother-in-law were hosting in their home.

We presented Abba with this possibility and were waiting for His will to be made known in the matter, largely because in order to make such a trip we needed a financial miracle, as at St. Vincent we were only paid a small stipend.

Amazingly, within a very short time money came in. It was all delivered by hand; some coming from people whom we didn't even know. What was especially puzzling was the form in which it came—Dutch, Swiss, French, English, German, American and Israeli currency.

To this day we do not quite understand how this came about, but at the time we felt that it was a signal from our God that our going was somehow connected to the revelation of the scattering of the tribes of Israel into many nations.

The work with our little group of "adopted" children was physically draining on Rimona. She really needed a rest. That rest came in a most surprising way, following a four kilometer (about two and a half mile) walk to the old monastery of St. John In The Desert.

We went there intending to buy goat cheese from the monks. As we entered the grounds, I saw a sign that said, "Beware Dog." Within a few steps of the sign, I noticed the dog looking at us and so stopped dead in my tracks, stretching out my hand to stop Rimona too.

We stood frozen for a second, and then I realized that although the animal was chained, we were inside the chain's perimeter. Although we attempted to retreat, it was to no avail. The dog charged at us and the next thing we knew he had punctured two holes in Rimona's leg.

After a trip to the hospital, Tetanus shots, bandages and painkillers, Rimona settled down for an extensive recuperation in our "cave." Not knowing whether to laugh or cry about our situation, we concluded that the incident at least afforded her a much-needed rest, and that with the full consent of the sisters.

Within a month or so we were making preparations to leave for the States, with the full knowledge that it was going to be very difficult to part with our little flock. But as the Father would have it we were blessed by the news that almost half of them were leaving for other places.

When we arrived in Wisconsin we were greeted lovingly, a fact that helped alleviate some of the sadness of departing from family, friends, and our beloved Land of Israel.

We almost immediately settled into making a temporary home for ourselves, thinking we would only be there for a year.

## A Conference

Within a week of our arrival a door opened for me to go to a conference in Georgia, with a possibility of sharing some of the things the Lord had been laying on my heart. I was excited at the opportunity of being able to tell people about what I was seeing concerning the identity and restoration of the lost tribes of Israel.

As it turned out, several of us went to the conference together. During one of the sessions it was decided by the leadership to let me share briefly about Israel. Just prior to that time my niece, Julie, sang "El Shaddai." The anointing that came over the audience was awe inspiring.

When I picked up the microphone, the air was electrified with God's presence. I knew that the message that was so much on His heart was not going to be delivered by my own strength.

As I shared from the words of the Prophets, there was much weeping. Their ancient words came alive with new meaning. Those who had deep longings in their Hebraic souls responded from deep within their hearts.

The Spirit seemed to rivet a connection in their spirits concerning the *LoAmi* ("Not My People") of Hosea chapter one; they began to understand the relationship between the Prophets' words and the Apostles' revelation of the identity of those called "sons of the living God," in both Hosea chapter one and Romans chapter eight.

I returned the microphone to one of the leaders, the musicians began to play a song, and that set two hundred or so congregants marching around the room singing:

"I want to see Israel marching; I want to hear the Kingdom call; I want to climb Zion's mountain, I want to see great Babylon fall; I want to see Jesus reigning upon

King David's royal throne. Oh won't that be a glorious sight to see when Israel comes marching home!"

Tears were flowing down my cheeks like rivers. I never knew that tear glands could produce so much water.

## A Surprise Telephone Call

Later that afternoon several people wanted to sit down and talk about the message. One of those was a young man by the name of John. The Father had already been speaking to him about the restoration of the Kingdom to Israel, and the place of the House of David in the scheme of things. He was living on a communal farm in Ohio, and as he wanted to stay in touch, he asked for my telephone number, which I gladly gave him.

At the time I did not know that within several weeks that number would not be valid.

Two or three weeks after returning home, we received a surprise telephone call from Angus and Batya Wootten, whom we had met in Israel almost two years earlier, but had had no contact with since then. Needless to say, we were very curious how they had found out that we were in the States. Batya then proceeded to tell us about a man named John from Ohio, who upon visiting a cousin living in the State of Maine happened to see on his desk one of their *House of David Herald* newsletters.

Being intrigued by the title, John started reading and became more and more interested. When John found out that the authors actually lived right along his route home, he decided to call on them.

While with them, John mentioned that he had met a fellow named Ephraim from Israel, and that they had discussed these very topics.

Batya's mouth just about dropped to the floor when she heard this news, and asked how she might contact us. John just happened to have the phone number that I had given him.

Amazingly, about an hour after we had spoken with our "Two House" friends, the telephone technicians came and disconnected the line!

Batya told us about the manuscript she was working on and that she and Angus would love to have us come and stay with them for a week and go through it together.

We, of course, were thrilled to have the opportunity. They graciously supplied us with the airline tickets, and Rimona, now almost eight months pregnant, and I were off to their beautiful home in upstate New York.

Our time with Angus and Batya was wonderful. Especially meaningful were the many hours we spent sharing revelation insights about our mutual interest, as well as sharing our personal testimonies.

Batya's manuscript, *In Search of Israel,* served as a great tool to keep us on track. Finding someone to talk to about these scriptural truths that we both were seeing was a tremendous blessing. All of us had for years felt a burning within from this gut-wrenching revelation. However, our time together made us feel as though we had discovered a welcome and lush oasis in the desert.

While helping Batya give birth to her first book on the subject of the Two Houses of Israel, we were reminded that we had a birthing of our own in the very near future. At this time we also were making preparations, such as meeting weekly with the midwife and going through a large quantity of reading materials.

## Our First Birth

I kept busy helping my sister in her home school, teaching beginning Hebrew to a class of about nine students. I was also occupied by going out to the woods and cutting firewood for the winter, and once a week I participated in a Bible teaching session with fifteen prisoners at the Federal Correctional Institution.

About two weeks before the due date, on a Shabbat morning, Rimona began to have a few extra pains. The day we had been waiting for had at last arrived.

The midwife came over and began to monitor her progress. My job was to wait until I was needed. Time seemed to slow to a stop. After about eight hours of progressive labor, I was called into action. The next four hours will live in my memory for the rest of my life.

There is nothing like sharing an experience of the birthing of new life! But for all the sharing in the world, there is only one who delivers!

My job entailed being with my wife when she needed me, and being ready to catch the little one upon arrival.

As Rimona's pains grew in intensity and frequency, it became almost unbearable for me to watch her go through the agony. At times I felt helpless; *"Oh God give her the grace!"* I would shout under my breath. Then, I felt the midwife pulling me gently by the arm and whispering, "You better get down there, the head is crowning."

As I positioned myself to catch the baby, I saw the top of the head, while the groaning of travail from the excruciating pain that Rimona was experiencing seemed to be muffled from my hearing. It was as if everything went into slow motion. The head soon came through, and in a matter of seconds a little human being landed in my hands, his head in the palm of my right hand and his bottom in the palm of my left.

The sight of two little black eyes staring up at me is forever etched in my memory. Time stopped as a father met his firstborn. Our gazes locked and we looked at each other as if we were meeting in some mysterious realm of oneness. I heard the midwife say, *"It's a boy!"*

I looked up and sure enough, she was right. Then I got up to hand the little guy to a waiting mother who was now half laughing and half crying.

Knowing how much Rimona likes cleanliness, I was amazed that she so willingly reached out and took the little naked body that was still covered with blood and lard-like white substance.

I watched as the mother of my son gently caressed her newborn. Her tears of joy brought me back to her side and both of us gave thanks with grateful hearts to a living God. The midwife then asked me if I wanted to cut the umbilical cord, which I gladly did.

While the midwife was washing the baby, Rimona got up and promptly went to the kitchen to make a call to her parents (we didn't own a cordless phone). They were waiting, feeling like they were sitting on pins and needles in Tel Aviv, Israel. Being their first grandchild, the occasion was especially joyous for them, as it was also coupled with the Feast of Succot, or Tabernacles, which had just begun.

## The Brit Milah

Finding a Mohel (one who performs circumcisions) and a place to hold the circumcision rite was somewhat challenging. When we failed to receive a response from the Orthodox synagogue in Madison, we contacted the Conservative one and arrangements were made for the circumcision of our firstborn son.

When the eighth day arrived ( which also happened to be the seventh of Succot), we had a gathering at my sister's house in the morning and we dedicated Yonatan ("God's Gift") to the Lord.

The Father tells us that all the firstborn belong to Him, and now my firstborn son was included in that number. Hallelujah!

During the dedication I read over Yonatan Psalm 139:1-16. I also blessed him with Psalm 20:1-5.

After some wonderful food and fellowship we were off to Madison to meet the Rabbi and the Mohel at the Beth Israel Center.

The Brit was an especially festive occasion filled with

God's presence. The Mohel was cheerful, and tried, with a variety of sounds, to pacify his patient, but the latter only rewarded him with a well aimed "fountain splatter."

It didn't take long to settle back into the routines of life in rural America. However, Rimona and I did feel a little like fish out of water. Our homeland was still Israel.

I continued teaching from the Scriptures in the community, as well as Hebrew, at the school. This brought in a little income, but not enough to pay the bills. At one time we had a forty-seven-dollar electric bill, which we couldn't cover. Then the clothes dryer, at my brother's house, where we were living, broke down.

I hoped to be able to fix the dryer myself and proceeded to check it out. As I opened the back and started looking inside I found a few coins. By the time I finished digging into the machine, I counted a little over forty-seven dollars worth of change. We were thankful for a dryer that was in working order again, and for the treasure that enabled us to pay the electric bill (although the dryer never yielded such riches again).

## Another Bundle of Joy!

Rimona's parents came to visit us for a couple of months. Since it soon appeared that we would not be coming back at the end of the one year, at the airport, before leaving for Israel, Rimona's dad pulled me aside. He asked me point blank if Rimona was pregnant again. I denied any such possibility, because she was still nursing Yonatan. To our surprise, a couple of weeks later we found out that indeed that was the case.

With the news of another child on the way, I had to look for a full time job, and a door opened almost immediately for me to work with handicapped adults at a sheltered workshop. The pay, however, barely met our monthly expenses. My dad graciously helped us out and bought us a nice used, medium size station wagon. The months were going by, and our next child was growing and active inside its mother's womb.

As for firstborn Yonatan, he was going on a year and a half and was full of mischief. The little guy was quite a handful for a pregnant Rimona. Then, one day at the end of April 1987, while at work, I broke a bone in my leg.

This was a painful experience, and, the following afternoon, Rimona announced that the day for the new arrival may have come.

Because this baby was late, and had given a few false signals before, Rimona felt a bit unsure about its arrival and hadn't made any special preparations. In fact, the house was unusually messy that evening. But when it seemed that the labor pains were becoming more frequent, we called both the midwife and my sister. A bulky Rimona was now trying to quickly put things away, to make the place more fitting for the occasion.

While her disabled husband was sitting in the living room, talking with our good friends who had come from Ohio to help us, Rimona was soaking herself in the bath. Then all of a sudden, she burst out of the bathroom running toward the bedroom—the midwife right behind her.

Passing me by, Chris (the midwife) said that if I were to catch this one, I'd better come in a hurry. Hopping on one leg I made it into the bedroom, and ten minutes later I was holding our little girl in the same position that I had held our son some seventeen months earlier.

However, this time it seemed my pain might be matching that which Rimona had just experienced. So as soon as I could, I settled down into a rocking chair with my new and beautiful daughter, whom we named Sehter-Hadar ("Hiding Place" and "Splendor").

Five years earlier, while on the kibbutz and trying to read Psalm 91 in Hebrew, I came across a word I couldn't pronounce. Rimona carefully enunciated it, "Seh-ter" and said it meant "secret," or "hiding place." I immediately said that it would make a beautiful name for a daughter. Rimona responded that it was not a known name, yet was equally persuaded. It portrayed a fitting picture of Israel's Husbandman hiding the seed of the forefathers in the womb of the earth, until the time would come for them to be revealed in the splendor of holiness.

Truly, I enjoyed the precious and splendorous moments with little Sehter-Hadar nestled in my arms.

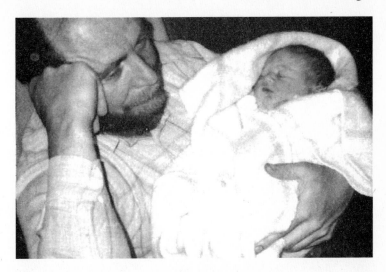

*Above)* Sehter-Hadar and her Abba (Daddy)
*Below)* Yonatan at two years and Sehter-Hadar at one.

# Return to the Land

Twenty-Two

# Traveling Around

My high school class of 1962 was celebrating our 25th year reunion, the first one I ever attended. The event was very interesting to say the least.

No one seemed to recognize me after 25 years. Some of my classmates were already grandparents, or had children in college, while I was the father of a one week old baby daughter and a year-and-half old son. Nonetheless, I received prizes for having come the farthest, Israel, and for being the one least recognized.

Now with two children, our hopes of returning to Israel seemed ever dimmer, as the responsibilities of parenting our own little flock took priority over everything else.

Soon after recovering from the broken leg, I went back to work. But things seemed different. I began to feel the tugging of the call to share the message of the Two Houses of Israel, but again the question loomed before us: *"Is this the right time to step out on the waters?"*

We had tried to share this truth that burned within us before, only to be met with some fiery opposition.

## Travels
The State of Florida came to the forefront of our consciousness. While we were still on the kibbutz, for no apparent reason, Rimona could not get Florida off her

mind. Now it seemed to us that there was a reason for that temporary fixation. The more we pondered the idea, the more we thought that perhaps this trip would launch us into full time ministry. Although without financial backing it was quite a risky proposition, especially now with two small children. When presenting the idea to family and friends they were cautious about giving their approval. Knowing us, they were not surprised that we eventually decided to take off, and that I gave notice at work with the hope of doing some traveling and teaching.

Sehter Hadar was six months old and Yonatan had just turned two, when we set out on our journey southward in the Fall of 1987. My sister had told us about a conference in Georgia, in the same place where I had shared about the Two Houses two years earlier.

I thought perhaps there would be an opportunity to share there again, but because the leadership perceived Israel as being only symbolic of the spiritual Body of Messiah, our message didn't fit. That door did not open for us again. However, we did make some contacts with others who lived in Florida, and were invited to visit them as we traveled through the state.

We spent almost two months driving the entire coastline of Florida, with prolonged stops in certain areas. One particular area where we stopped once on the way down, and again on the way back, was Orlando, Kissimmee / Saint Cloud.

Years later, when Angus and Batya felt led to move their House of David / Messianic Israel Ministries to that area, we pondered the connection. As far as we were aware, the trip to Florida did not yield any fruit, but we did sow a few seeds.

Although our speculations and attempts may not have lined up with what Abba was doing at the time, we still know that, as Believers, we all embrace a mystery that is at work in us at all times, whether we are aware of it or not.

Since that time we have learned that we, in and of ourselves, are not the focus. Instead, the God of Israel and His faithfulness to the covenants that He made with our forefathers should be the focus of our attention. For this reason, no matter where we go, His life, which is in us, is being borne right along. What He does, right then and there, or in the future, is totally by His will, and is executed by His Spirit and by our obedience and willingness to participate in His divine plan.

Our Florida trip came to an abrupt halt when we ran out of money. The little that we had left was only sufficient to get us back to Wisconsin. Nonetheless, the Father was faithful to show us in a dream that we were to go back there, as well as to point us to a very clear word from Scripture. It said simply: "Flee from this place!"

In the dream we were all in a boat on a pond, but the water began to freeze up and the only open channel was back on my parents' shore, where my family was standing. We arrived from our trip in the first part of December, and within a week I returned to my old job, as no one else was hired in the interim. With no money to return to Israel, we settled down for a long winter's nap.

The year was filled with life experiences as a family, which the Lord used to shape and mold His vessels. One such occasion concerned my relationship with my daughter. I was busy reading my Bible one morning when she happened to be crawling in from the kitchen to the living room. As I glanced down, I felt the Spirit convicting me of neglecting her. I put the Bible down and picked her up, holding her close. With tears in my eyes I asked her to forgive me. She may have been only a baby, but we experienced a deep reconciliation and a healing.

Almost a year went by from the time we had returned from Florida. I was driving home from work one afternoon when a car with three teenagers drove through a stop sign at high speed and struck the front left side of my car, sending me spinning.

After coming to, I got out of the car to see what had happened to the passengers of the other vehicle. Then I noticed that one side of my head was about twice its normal size, while the three passengers were unharmed.

I also saw that the front end of my car was totally smashed in. Nevertheless, I was very thankful to the Lord, for if there had been another millisecond's delay, their car would have hit the door on the driver's side, which could have marked the end of my life.

The good news is that the insurance company offered us a settlement that payed our way home.

Within a few months of the accident, we had in hand enough money to buy our tickets back to Israel, send some of the belongings that we accumulated over the four years in a shipping crate, pay off bills, and even have a little left over.

By the end of March 1989, with five suitcases, two children and about five hundred dollars, we were saying our good-byes and flying back to our homeland, to beloved Israel.

Twenty-Three

# The Mounts of Blessing and Curse

Rimona's parents welcomed us with great joy. They opened their small one bedroom apartment that we might temporary settle in with them.

The six of us were a little cramped, but seemed to manage. Rimona and I spent almost two months in government agencies and bureaus, getting ourselves settled back into the country. We began to see many signs in the form of small miracles that daily welcomed us home.

One such divine path presented itself when someone in a government agency told me to get into the work force immediately, and not study or take courses in Hebrew. Teaching jobs seemed to be out of the question, because of my language problem. However, one day I ran into an old acquaintance. She was a friend from my years at Project Kibbutz, and she told me about an institution for the retarded in Hertzliyah called Levtzeler, where caretakers were needed. I called and made arrangements for an interview with one of the directors. Two days later, when I arrived at the beautiful facility, I mentioned to the director that I was actually a special education teacher and that I loved working with these children. Since there was a need for workers, the interview was merely a formality. But the Lord had other ideas...

After showing us the facility, we walked into the office of the director of the adjoining government school. The director was in a panic, as one of his teachers, who was seven months pregnant, was in the hospital suffering from certain complications. He had an urgent need for a teacher, for at least a month and a half until the end of the school year. The director of the institution told him not to worry, as there was one standing in the office!

The following day I started working in the school as a substitute teacher, in a classroom of low-level multi-handicapped teenagers. The Lord was moving heaven and earth in all levels of immigrant absorption and the educational system to secure a salary and a job for me.

I was not, however, guaranteed a job for the following year, as the original teacher had the right to return to her classroom. But again, things did not work out for her, as the baby that was born had some physical difficulties and she was allowed a year's leave to take care of her family. I was asked to stay on, and so in the following year I began working in a full time teaching position.

A short time after starting work at the school we heard of a family of Believers who lived not far from there, and who were looking for someone to house-sit for two months. This was another one of those little divine arrangements that gave us some space to begin to live a little bit more comfortably.

After the two months of grace were up, we had to find our own apartment to rent, and a family from the congregation we attended told us about theirs. It was located in a Sharon Valley town called Kfar Sabba. This family had to leave the country within a short time and was looking for someone to rent it.

We immediately felt this was our answer to prayer. Without seeing it we agreed to take it.

The two bedroom apartment was perfect for our little family.

## The Sharon Valley

Rimona's parents informed us that they would like to help us out with the purchase of an apartment somewhere in the area. Their savings were limited, so we hunted and hunted for a place within the desired amount. Rimona's father became sick during this time and was in and out of the hospital for more than two years. In the interim, we were still looking to buy something permanent, and came very close to closing deals, but the Father always seemed to block the way when we tried to purchase any of the houses or apartments that we looked at in and around the region that we now called home—the Sharon Valley.

We had discussed with Rimona's parents the possibility of buying or building a house in the so-called "West Bank," but to them that was out of the question. They felt that it was too dangerous and financially risky. That land could be given over to the Palestinians at some point in the future. We therefore dismissed the idea.

However, door after door kept closing on us.

One day Rimona and I decided to drive across the "Green Line" and check out a couple of settlements that were not more than a few kilometers into the territories. They were very close to Kfar Sabba, which is where we were living at the time, but what we looked at did not appeal to us. Then, around Succot of 1989, Rimona heard over the radio that a special housing campaign was underway in the settlement of Alfe Menashe (again, very close to where we were living in Kfar Sabba). We decided to look it over.

## Alfe Menashe

The settlement was located just beyond a large Arab city called Kalkiliya, and on the way to Shechem. The area was already noted for a terrorist attack that had taken place nearby a few years beforehand, in which a pregnant mother and one of her other children were killed on the road leading to the settlement.

As we drove through the town, the beauty of the location pleasantly surprised us. Then we turned down a rocky road into an area that was just beginning to be developed. Suddenly both of us were filled with an assurance that this would be our home. When we inquired at the development office we were told that there were only three lots left, and one had already been spoken for.

After viewing the lots we picked the one that we liked the best, but found that it was the one that had been taken. In order for the deal to go through an answer had to be given the following day, so we drove to the hospital where we met Rimona's parents.

After some conversation that led nowhere, I felt to ask her father what was the difference between when he came to Israel, back in 1935, and today's conditions in Samaria. Somehow Abba used that question to convince Rimona's parents—that is, along with the idea that the amount of money we would need to be able to buy an old two-bedroom apartment elsewhere, would suffice to build a four-bedroom villa on a quarter acre of land.

Concurrently, a report came of a hand grenade thrown on a street near their home in downtown Tel Aviv, and although it turned out to be a dud, it was enough for them to realize that the danger of terror attacks lurked everywhere.

The following day we were up early for the journey to the development office in Alfe Menashe. The name, Alfe Menashe, is from Moses' blessing to Joseph. For Moses says in Deuteronomy 33:17: "As the first born of his ox, majesty is his, and his horns are the horns of the wild ox; with them he shall push the peoples, all at once, to the ends of the earth, and those are the ten thousands of Ephraim, and those are the thousands of Menashe."

Since it was situated in Menashe's territory, the

settlement was given the name "The Thousands of Menashe."

Although the lot that we felt we were supposed to have in Alfe Menashe had already been spoken for, we soon found that the people decided to take the property behind us, as they did not want to be at the edge of the settlement, in spite of the absolutely beautiful panoramic view.

We stopped at the lot that had been our first choice, and looked out over the hills and ravines of Samaria. Giving thanks, we read Ezekiel chapter 36:

"And you, son of man, prophesy to the mountains of Israel and say, 'O mountains of Israel, hear the word of God. Thus says the Lord God, Because the enemy has spoken against you, "Aha!" and, "The everlasting heights have become our possession," therefore prophesy and say..."For good reason they have made you desolate and crushed you from every side, that you would become a possession of the rest of the nations and you have been taken up in the talk and the whispering of the people.'" Therefore, O mountains of Israel, hear the word of the Lord God....to the mountains and to the hills, to the ravines and to the valleys, to the desolate wastes and to the forsaken cities which have become a prey and a derision to the rest of the nations which are round about...Surely in the fire of My jealousy I have spoken against the rest of the nations, and against all Edom, who appropriated My land for themselves as a possession with wholehearted joy and with scorn of soul, to drive it out for a prey. Therefore prophesy concerning the land of Israel and say to the mountains and to the hills, to the ravines and to the valleys, 'Thus says the Lord God, Behold, I have spoken in My jealousy and in My wrath because you have endured the insults of the nations. Therefore...I have sworn that surely the nations which are around you will themselves endure their insults. But you, O mountains of Israel, you will put forth your branches and bear your fruit for My people Israel; for they will soon come. For, behold, I am for you, and I will turn to you, and you will be cultivated and sown. I will multiply men on you, all the house of Israel, all of it; and the cities will be inhabited and the waste places will be rebuilt. I will multiply on you man and beast; and they will increase and be fruitful; and I will cause you to be inhabited as you were formerly and will treat you better than at the first. Thus you will know that I am the Lord. Yes, I will cause men—My people Israel—to walk on you and possess you, so that you will become their inheritance and never again bereave them of children'" (Ezekiel 36:1-12).

## The Privilege...

Our eyes filled with tears as we read the Lord's word to the mountains, hills, ravines and valleys that lay before our eyes. We felt so blessed, so privileged to think we would soon be looking on this view through the windows of our new home.

A few days later we received a call from Angus and Batya. They had brought a group of Believers to Israel for the Feast of Tabernacles. We told them of our purchase in the settlement and they immediately wanted to come and see it for themselves. A day or so later we picked them up and brought them to the settlement.

## Like a Tree that is Planted

As we were standing there, looking toward the Mounts of Blessing and Curse that lay before us, Batya's eyes fell on a small olive tree next to the road. Her eyes lit up as she broke a branch from that tree and together we stuck it in the ground on our property, as a sign of the union of the "two sticks" of Judah and Ephraim.

Together, with our voices being carried by the Spirit over the ancient mountains of our forefathers, we read aloud Ezekiel 37:15-22 and Hosea 1:10-11.

"The word of the Lord came again to me saying, 'And you, son of man, take for yourself one stick and write on it, "For Judah and for the sons of Israel, his companions," then take another stick and write on it, "For Joseph, the stick of Ephraim and all the house of Israel, his companions." Then join them for yourself one to another into one stick, that they may become one in your hand.

"And when the sons of your people speak to you saying; 'Will you not declare to us what you mean by these?' say to them, "Thus says the Lord God, 'Behold, I will take the stick of Joseph, which is in the hand of Ephraim, and the tribes of Israel, his companions; and I will put them with it, with the stick of Judah, and make them one stick, and they will be one in My hand....I will take the sons of Israel from among the nations where they have gone, and I will gather them from every side and bring them into their own land; and I will make them one nation in the land, on the mountains of Israel; and one king will be king for all of them; and they will no longer be two nations, and they will no longer be divided into two kingdoms.

"'And they will no longer defile themselves with their idols, or with their detestable things, or with any of their transgressions....And they will be My people, and I will be their God....They will all have one shepherd....and I will... set My sanctuary in their midst forever. My dwelling place also will be with them; and I will be their God, and they will be My people"'" (Ezekiel 37:16-27).

"Yet the number of the sons of Israel will be like the sand of the sea, which cannot be measured or numbered; and in the place where it is said to them, 'You are not My people,' it will be said to them, 'You are the sons of the living God.' And the sons of Judah and the sons of Israel will be gathered together, and they will appoint for themselves one leader, and they will go up from the land, for great will be the day of Jezreel'" (Hosea 1:10-11).

# Return to the Land

The four of us celebrated all the way back up to Jerusalem...

Twenty-Four

# Building and Bombs

Once the contracts were signed, our next challenge was to find an honest contractor.

We did a lot of praying about this, and then heard about a Believer who quit the business because of the corruption in the building trade. He eventually agreed to build our house, albeit with a lot of reservations.

He warned us that it would cost us a lot more than what we had actually planned for, as he would not by pass government regulations and required fees. We totally concurred with his decision, and felt that God would bless the work of his hands.

On the Shabbat just before work was to start on our house, we had a special prayer time in the congregation. Since our contractor was a member of the same fellowship, all three of us were called up for prayer. As soon as the prayer was over, one of the elders' wives, who was not noted for supporting our "Two Houses Theory" (to put it mildly), spoke out and said very emphatically to the pastor: "Now is the time to sing Jeremiah 31."

This song cites some of the first verses of the chapter, mentioning the planting of vineyards in Samaria and the watchmen who cry out "let us go up to Zion."

Although familiar with the song, we have not heard it sung publicly anywhere before nor since.

We took the song as personal word of encouragement and confirmation of our vision, of the return of the House of Ephraim to Samaria, in the very the location that the Father had chosen for our home. If we needed further assurance as to our move, there it was, and coming from a very unlikely source at that!

## Jeremiah 31

"At that time," declares the Lord, "I will be the God of all the families of Israel, and they shall be My people." Thus says the Lord, The people who survived the sword found grace in the wilderness—Israel, when it went to find its rest. The Lord appeared to him from afar, saying, "I have loved you with an everlasting love; Therefore I have drawn you with lovingkindness. Again I will build you and you will be rebuilt, O virgin of Israel! Again you will take up your tambourines, and go forth to the dances of the merrymakers. Again you will plant vineyards on the hills of Samaria; the planters will plant and will enjoy them. For there will be a day when watchmen on the hills of Ephraim call out, 'Arise, and let us go up to Zion, to the Lord our God.' For thus says the Lord, 'Sing aloud with gladness for Jacob, and shout among the chief of the nations; proclaim, give praise and say, 'O Lord, save Your people, the remnant of Israel.'

"Behold, I am bringing them from the north country, and I will gather them from the remote parts of the earth, among them the blind and the lame, the woman with child and she who is in labor with child, together; a great company, they will return here. With weeping they will come, and by supplication I will lead them; I will make them walk by streams of waters, on a straight path in which they will not stumble; for I am a father to Israel, and Ephraim is My firstborn.

"Hear the word of the Lord, O nations, and declare in the coastlands afar off, and say, "He who scattered Israel will gather him and keep him as a shepherd keeps his flock. For the Lord has ransomed Jacob and redeemed

him from the hand of him who was stronger than he.
They will come and shout for joy on the height of Zion,
and they will be radiant over the bounty of the Lord
—over the grain and the new wine and the oil, and over
the young of the flock and the herd; and their life will be
like a watered garden, and they will never languish
again.

"Then the virgin will rejoice in the dance, and the
young men and the old, together, for I will turn their
mourning into joy and will comfort them and give them
joy for their sorrow. I will fill the soul of the priests with
abundance, and My people will be satisfied with My
goodness," declares the Lord.

"Thus says the Lord, 'A voice is heard in Ramah,
lamentation and bitter weeping. Rachel is weeping for
her children; she refuses to be comforted for her children,
because they are no more."

"Thus says the Lord, "Restrain your voice from
weeping and your eyes from tears; for your work will be
rewarded," declares the Lord, and they will return from
the land of the enemy. There is hope for your future,
declares the Lord, and your children will return to their
own territory.

"I have surely heard Ephraim grieving, 'You have
chastised me, and I was chastised, like an untrained calf;
bring me back that I may be restored, for You are the
Lord my God. For after I turned back, I repented; and
after I was instructed, I smote on my thigh; I was
ashamed and also humiliated because I bore the reproach
of my youth.'

"Is Ephraim My dear son? Is he a delightful child?
Indeed, as often as I have spoken against him, I certainly
still remember him; therefore My heart yearns for him;
I will surely have mercy on him," declares the Lord.

"Set up for yourself roadmarks, place for yourself
guideposts; direct your mind to the highway, the way by
which you went. Return, O virgin of Israel, return to

these your cities.

"How long will you go here and there, O faithless daughter? For the Lord has created a new thing in the earth—a woman will encompass a man."

"Thus says the Lord of hosts, the God of Israel, 'Once again they will speak this word in the land of Judah and in its cities when I restore their fortunes, 'The Lord bless you, O abode of righteousness, O holy hill!' Judah and all its cities will dwell together in it, the farmer and they who go about with flocks. For I satisfy the weary ones and refresh everyone who languishes....'" (Jeremiah 31:1-25).

## War

The work on our home commenced in August of 1990. And it was not an easy time in the building industry. One needed a lot of patience to wait for materials and to work through labor strikes.

Because of terrorist activity, the roads in some areas were closed intermittently, thus preventing the Palestinian construction workers from showing up at their jobs.

We knew it would not be long before the American coalition would make its move on Iraq, and that the latter would retaliate by an attack on Israel.

We longed to be in our new home, but were still living in Kfar Sabba, which was near Tel Aviv, and thus just might be within the target zone of Scud attacks. All in all, very little work was done on the house during the American war in Iraq.

In the meantime our government was preparing for this eventuality, and was expecting an attack of biological and chemical warheads. We all received our gas masks, and the smaller children were equipped with little plastic tents. We were instructed to seal off one of the bedrooms in the house with plastic sheets over the windows and foam rubber strips around the doors. We also had to have an ample supply of water and food.

# Building and Bombs

A little after midnight, on January fifteenth, 1991, our telephone rang. It was a friend from our congregation who was actually living in Alfe Menashe. She informed us that the United States was bombing Baghdad.

We turned on the television to watch the blow-by-blow accounts, as the night skies around that Iraqi capital lit up with the fires of war. It wasn't long after that, that our own sirens began to wail with the impending sounds of giant explosions coming from somewhere in the Tel-Aviv area.

At the first sound of the sirens I ran into the children's bedroom and carried our son to the sealed room; unfortunately for him I banged his head on the door as we passed through it. I ran back and brought our sleeping daughter and laid her in her protective tent.

We no sooner closed the door when the sound of the explosions pierced the late night air. We were lying in our bed looking at each other through our gas masks. It was like being in a room with aliens.

The radio was giving the reports of the damage incurred in Tel-Aviv. Tension was high as we waited to hear from Rimona's parents who lived in the center of the city. We prayed earnestly for their safety.

In the two months of the war, thirty-nine Scud missiles fell on Israeli towns, with huge amounts of damage to buildings and property. Amazingly, no lives were lost, although people were told not to go to their bomb shelters but to stay in the sealed rooms.

Throughout the whole country stories of miracle after miracle were being recounted, about how people were saved or spared from certain death. Even our otherwise cynical media deigned to report them, along with relevant Scriptures, while giving credit to the One who was orchestrating all of this

One such episode occurred in an apartment complex where people were confused as to whether to go for protection in the bomb shelter, as all the Scuds up to that point had conventional bombs, or to stay in their sealed rooms. One night when the sirens wailed, twenty of the residents decided to go to the shelter but could not find the key to unlock the door.

They returned to their apartments and waited for the blast. And this particular time the Scud fell right on top of their bomb shelter and destroyed it. Had they been inside, they would all have perished. This was another sign from the Almighty that He was watching over the people whom He chose so long ago.

## Semblance of Normalcy?

After weathering the storm of the Scud attacks, we settled back down to completing the building process of our home.

Those days seemed to be characterized by some semblance of normalcy, but of course in Israel you can't second-guess what may happen at any given moment.

For instance, you might go to the mailbox and find a letter of induction into the army...

Twenty-Five

# Life in the Land

Being introduced into the Israeli Defense Forces at this time in my life seemed like poor timing from my point of view. Nonetheless, six weeks of basic training were destined to be my lot with the IDF.

For someone who had served in the American Army twenty-three years earlier, going through army physicals was not a new experience, but in this case it was especially interesting. Our bravery was put to the test when we had to drop our drawers in front of a young eighteen-year-old female medic, who dipped to the right and then to the left.

Red faces and all, the day came when all of us new recruits were to meet and be bused to our new home, somewhere on the mountains in Samaria. It was a beautiful location north of Jerusalem, but a little cold, as we were still in late March (of 1991).

Our particular company was made up of new immigrants in their late thirties and forties, from twenty different nations, mostly Russians with a limited vocabulary of Hebrew.

My heart went out to the Ethiopians, as they were put together with very experienced Russian officers who also had to start out as privates. The Ethiopians literally did not know their right hand from their left, let alone which end of the gun to use. They also did not know Hebrew, while the Russians, of course, communicated with one another in their own language. It was obvious that the Russians were making fun of these poor Ethiopian men.

I often wondered what went through the mind of our nineteen-year-old female drill sergeant, as she tried to get us to comply with some disciplinary measures that are typical of boot camp. It was a wonder that no lives were lost during those six weeks, as we all had the potential of acting pretty foolishly.

Being a former American soldier from the sixties, I got to meet, face to face, my ex-Russian counterparts, right in the next bunk. We had some interesting conversations about our military experiences, which were not that different. I found out from my new compatriots that during the 1982 Lebanon War, the Russians were poised to back the Syrians if Israel had gone into the Baka Valley where the Syrian strongholds were situated.

According to this former Russian officer, the Russian Army had missiles with nuclear warheads aimed at Israel, along with troops and equipment ready to enter into a full-scale war against us. The United States was served with an ultimatum, which meant that the latter either had to stop the Israeli incursion into Lebanon, or face the consequence of a war in the Middle East.

In spite of the American alliance with Israel, the U.S. was not willing to risk its oil interests in the region, as the rest of the Arab nations were backing the Syrians and the Russians. The President of the United States at that time therefore made sure that Israel would pull back. Thus the genocide of Lebanese Christians continued until Lebanon became another Islamic state.

After my basic training my Heavenly Abba spared me from having to do reserve duty, as the reserve officer determined that I was too old to continue in the army.

## A Redesigned Blessing
Our house in Samaria was almost finished. A couple

of major mistakes and oversights on the part of the contractor actually turned out to be a blessing.

We found that even as Abba wants to "redesign" both Houses of Israel, so He truly redesigned our house.

In August of 1991 we moved most of our belongings into our new home, and we began to live in the place which the Spirit had confirmed to our hearts eight years prior. It had come to pass even as we thought it would while we were still living on the kibbutz back in the summer of 1984: "Then Rehoboam went to Shechem, for all Israel came to Shechem."

At the time that we received this word, we both felt that we were called to the heartland of Israel, somewhere near Shechem. Now here we were, blessed beyond belief, looking out of our front window at the mountains of Ebal and Gerizim, with a portion of the large Arab city of Shechem peeking out between the two.

We were quite amazed, as neither one of us had remembered that word of promise until the time came to select our lot two years earlier.

## The Twin Branched Olive Tree

Whereas the house was almost finished, the yard continued to be a mass of rocks and stones. Then one afternoon on my way to work (in addition to my teaching position I had a part time job working with a young man in a mental institution), my eye caught a large truck laden with twelve rather large olive tree trunks.

The truck was parked by a plant nursery and I walked over to inquire about purchasing one or two of them. The driver directed me to the owner of the nursery.

After some haggling, I paid the price for the trunk of my choice, and the driver agreed to deliver it to the house. As it had been cut off just below the ground, with one large protruding root, I was somewhat concerned about whether it would grow on its new site. The top part of the tree was not much more impressive either, as it had only two main branches no longer than the root, which stuck out from its gnarly looking trunk.

It was because of its impressive looking trunk, which disclosed its age of sixty odd years, that I had picked that particular specimen in the first place.

Upon its delivery with a lift arm, I asked the driver how to ensure that it would grow. "Just put some dirt around it and water it," was his short answer.

The soil was very rocky, and I couldn't dig a pit deep enough for its root to be buried in, so I propped it up. Then I asked one of my neighbors who was unloading topsoil to his own yard if I could buy from him a couple of tractor scoops of soil.

Our olive tree with the two stumpy limbs was the first plant to be placed in the ground of our property.

At Passover that year my mother and sister came to visit. My sister, being a gardener, couldn't wait to buy some plants and trees and start filling the yard with life, which by then had been covered with top soil.

Today, our once gnarly olive tree flourishes and yields fruit every year. It is planted where Angus and Batya and Rimona and I once believed in faith that Ephraim was now returning to his own soil—and Judah was welcoming him home.

## The Pillow Picture

One Shabbat, shortly after moving to Alfe Menashe, as we were driving back from our congregational gathering, we first smelled and then saw smoke rising from the back seat of our car.

I was using my father-in-law's 1973 VW Beetle, which once had a similar fire under the backseat. After that first episode, I covered the battery and the electrical outlets with a piece of a rubber inner tube as a safety precaution.

On this particular day we were giving a ride to a friend and her baby daughter. When I realized what was happening, I pulled over to the side of the road. All six of us piled out of the car.

I hurriedly took the back seat out and found that the rubber piece I had draped over the battery had caught on fire. With flames shooting up, I looked for something that would extinguish the blaze. Not wanting to use a jacket that was lying in the back, I grabbed a pillow that I had been using for back support and pressed it down on the burning rubber.

After putting out the blaze and airing the car a bit, we all got back in and continued our journey to our home in Alfe Menashe.

The friend's husband was already waiting anxiously for us at the house. While Rimona was telling him the story of our unexpected fire, I went out to fetch what was still left in the car, along with the blackened cushion. As I looked at the cloth, I noticed something unusual about the charred "design" that had been formed on it.

I called my seven-year-old son over and asked him what he saw; he immediately said "ee'sh" (man). I then showed it to our guests, and we all stood in amazement at what our God had painted with fire and rubber.

On the grey-beige cushion there appeared the face of a bearded man, with "Semitic" features. His head was draped with a headdress that flowed below the beard line. In the middle of the forehead, there was a depiction of what seemed like intertwined twigs that were twisted together. But what was most striking about his face, were the compassionate eyes which were gazing downward.

Truly, our Messiah was watching over us...

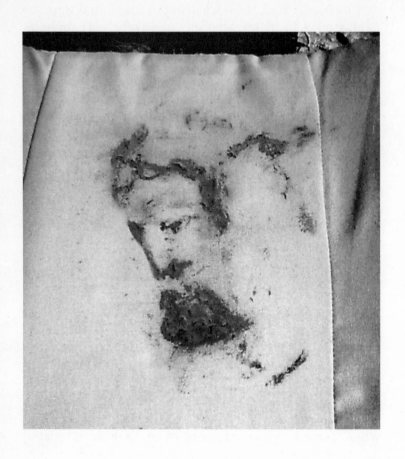

The grey-beige cushion
that was thrown over the fire in the car.
Truly, our Messiah watches over us.

The Twin Branched Olive Tree
Ephraim and Judah
Replanted in the Land

# Return to the Land

## Twenty-Six

# A New Reality

I now faced a new challenge, as the pastor and elders in our congregation became quite cold toward us because of our belief in the Two Houses of Israel.

For two years I had been the key person and the chairman of the congregation. That is, I was the one to open all the doors to the various rooms and amenities and to set up chairs. One day I spent about three hours going through the Scriptures with the pastor, showing him the plan of redemption as it was laid out in the Tanach (Old Testament), which of course includes the plan of the God of Jacob for His people: Israel and Judah.

His comment at the end was, "What good is it? So what if there are these two groups, or houses; now there is no Jew or Gentile, we are all one new man in Messiah."

A few weeks later at a congregational meeting, the pastor laid out the vision for the congregation, and added, in a polite way, that those who did not share that vision should either start their own congregation or find another.

Both Rimona and I felt confirmation in our spirits that these were our marching orders out of that fellowship.

Leaving the congregation brought us into a new reality, as far as fellowship was concerned. We were certain that some of the long time friends that we had while in the congregation would maintain relationships with us, but much to our surprise no one seemed to make the effort to continue doing so outside the framework of the organized system.

This caused us to review the genuineness of the relationships that were formed within that establishment. The Father did, however, find for us others who had similar experiences.

Soon relationships started forming with other Believers and we began meeting in our homes. The meetings were mainly centered on healing of old wounds, renewing our minds, and on the importance of healthy family relationships.

This was a growing time for us, as we were being prepared for our calling. It didn't seem to matter that the others were not necessarily open to the Two House teaching. Besides, after the conversation with the pastor and his nonchalant comment— "What good is it, and so what if there are these two groups, or houses; now there is no Jew or Gentile, we are all one new man in Messiah" —even I was perplexed about the relative importance of this revelation. Others were also of the opinion that today's Jews make up the union of the Two Houses.

Although my mind was reeling with doubts, my heart was still burning with the same intensity of revelation understanding that had been kindled in me ten years previously. I did, nonetheless, prayerfully request an answer to the pastor's comment.

Before long the Father gave me a very short reply: *"What good is it to know of My faithfulness to the covenants with your forefathers?"*

This had to have been His voice, as it is typically congruous with Hebraic thinking to answer a question with another question.

At the same time, one of the scriptural songs that I was taught back in the early seventies came flooding back into my memory: "I will sing of the mercies of the Lord forever; and with my mouth will I make known Your faithfulness to all generations" (Psalm 89:1, NKJV).

I had to ask myself: "Faithfulness to whom? To what? When? Where?"

Little by little, line upon line, the Spirit began to guide me into more and more truth about this testimony of His faithfulness and His mercies.

When I opened my Bible to Psalm 89 again, the following verses came alive: "For I have said, 'Mercy shall be built up forever; Your faithfulness You shall establish in the very heavens'" (89:2).

The same was true for Psalm 89:5 and 8 "And the heavens will praise Your wonders, O Lord; Your faithfulness also in the assembly of the called out ones," and "O Lord, Who is mighty like You? Your faithfulness also surrounds You."

Another of the Father's answers further clarified the who, what and when of my questioning. He directed me to read 1 Chronicles 16:8-36, and as a second scriptural witness, Psalm 105:1-15.   It became evident what the Lord was after.

He wanted to have His people in this generation become witnesses of His faithfulness to the covenant that He Himself swore to Abraham, Isaac and Jacob, especially as His judgments seemed to be drawing closer and closer.

I began to gain an understanding as to why we had to know His faithfulness in the context of His plans for the redemption of the creation.

This knowledge will be most necessary in helping us to survive the periods of tribulation that are destined to occur while our God shakes up the kingdoms of this world, and at the same time, begins to establish the restored eternal Kingdom to Israel.

## A New Understanding

With this understanding my prayer life began to change.  I understood that it was not just an issue of Believers becoming aware of their Israelite identity. Rather, it was a matter of our comprehending the connection of the Commonwealth of Israel to the establishment of God's Kingdom on this earth through a people.

Our next three years would be spent seeking first His Kingdom and His righteousness.

My work as a teacher in the special education system did not yield enough finances to support the needs of the family, so I took up other part time jobs, while Rimona was busy as a Hebrew translator. This meant that the only time available to study and read Scriptures was at 4:30 in the morning. I will never regret doing this, as at that time I felt as though I was going out to get manna, which was like the dew upon the ground, and had to be gathered before the sun came up.

The Tanach (First Covenant/Old Testament) became like a treasury, full of precious revelation truths, pearls of great price that were not to be squandered for personal gain, nor to be sold in the marketplace of a Babylonian religious system. Yeshua said: "Go rather to the lost sheep of the house of Israel. And as you go, preach, saying, 'The kingdom of God [heaven] is at hand...' Freely you have received, freely give" (Matthew 10:6-7, NKJV).

As the teaching year of 1996-97 drew near, I discovered that it was supposed to be my sabbatical, which meant that I could take a year off for study. My request, however, was turned down, as teachers with more seniority had first priority. My turn would come the following year, which I felt would also be used somehow for "ministry."

## Confirmation

The year of 1996 brought about a number of changes in our lives, one of which was to join a brother who had just started a congregation in the Tel-Aviv area. The Father had laid it on my heart to walk alongside him and assist him in whatever way possible. Rimona and I did a lot of praying about this involvement, as it had all the earmarks of an organized religious fellowship. Nevertheless, the pressure kept coming from the Spirit, so we ultimately yielded to it, as the home group meetings came to an end sometime beforehand.

The first confirmation to this commitment came when the pastor, in an early morning prayer meeting in which only the two of us were present, asked my forgiveness for the way the leadership in the Land had treated us. I was overwhelmed and wept at this gesture of reconciliation. I was still not sure why the Father wanted us involved again in building another congregation, possibly because it still took the form of a small meeting in a coffee house and had home-group Bible studies.

These meetings also yielded some very unexpected confirmations and prophetic words that ultimately led us into our present work. Three of those confirmations came through words of knowledge and prophetic utterances from three individuals who had come from overseas.

All of them had the same word, while none of them knew us, or each other. The words were simple and direct: "You are in the right place at the right time." There were also other words spoken over us during that period.

1996 was also a special year in other respects, as there were signs in the heavens that indicated change. There were two blood moons on two of the Lord's feast days, Passover and Succot, and the Hale Bop Comet lit up the night skies for almost a month between Purim and Passover. In addition, there was an appearance of a blue moon.

We began to see the evidence of these signs in the very message that had been in our hearts for over fifteen years. The Holy Spirit began to sovereignly increase this revelation in the hearts of His people all over the world. However, even before that significant year of 1996, there were several confirmations from unexpected sources.

One time the pastor referred to above, whom I later joined, brought to our house a lady evangelist from the U.S. and a guest from India.

When the guests walked in, Rimona just happened to be in the process of making chutney (a favorite Indian relish, which she had never made before or since). The guests had not been in the house for more than five minutes, when the man from India began to share with me about the Two Houses and the Gospel from Abraham.

I was struck in amazement when he told me that they had a Bible school in the center of India where they taught this way. This man did not know us, or anything about us before he came into the house.

A year later, during Succot, we were at a gathering and Rimona specifically asked me *not* to talk about the Two House issues, so as not to antagonize anyone. Well, as soon as we walked through the door, being determined not to blow our cover, someone I had never met before walked up to me and asked, *"What do you know about the Two Houses of Israel?"*

This was just the beginning, as reports continued coming of Believers' growing interest in the roots of their faith.

## A Final Decision

In the spring of 1997 I had to make a final decision on whether to take my sabbatical year, with pay or without. It would have been nice to have a full year's salary, but for that to take place I was required to participate in courses that I knew would just be a waste of time and resources. Besides, the desire to share the message of the restoration of God's Kingdom to Israel was growing in my heart.

However, I had to face the question, "What do I do for income?" My school salary for the previous year was supposed to finish by the end of August, and I had to make my decision by the end of March, five months ahead of that date. Needless to say, the whole family was in prayer over the matter.

Talk of our decision brought lots of advice on how to raise money. The pastor of our congregation even gave me hundreds of addresses of Messianic and Evangelical congregations that he had collected. He thought I should introduce myself to them. Although we were appreciative of the advice and the list, every time we went before the Father we felt Him say, "Do not go that way, I will take care of you!"

I could just hear my loving brothers and sisters quoting from 1 Timothy 5:8, "If anyone does not provide for his own, and especially for those of his household, he has denied the faith, and is worse than an unbeliever."

# Return to the Land

Twenty-Seven

# Being About
# the Father's Business

Eventually, I received what I thought was Yeshua's answer to our inquiry: "I want you to be about My Father's business!"

These words were somewhat puzzling, as we were thinking in terms of ministry and not business. A word of confirmation came when the Spirit brought back to my mind a Scripture that had impacted me greatly back in the days of Project Kibbutz (1978-1979).

At the time we had to memorize a list of verses from various parts of the Bible. I meditated on one from 1 Corinthians 15:58: "Therefore, my beloved brethren, be steadfast, immovable always abounding in the work *of* the Lord, knowing that your labor is not in vain in the Lord."

The little word "of" stood out to me like a sore thumb. My curiosity was aroused and I had to ask the question, "What is the work *of* the Lord? What is it that You are doing?" I had felt that many were working *for* the Lord, but was it the work *of* the Lord?

After that scriptural confirmation I prayerfully asked another question, "What do You mean by *'business'?*"

The answer came rather abruptly, "Don't worry about compensation, just do what I'm telling you to do."

This thought also lined up with what I heard Rimona

pray one morning:

"Abba, if we have to spend our time and energy raising money, I do not even want to begin walking this path!"

She had my agreement. We had seen enough abuse in the area of ministry financing, so the decision had to be made to do it God's way or not at all, and that meant that we were not to be concerned over these issues.

Upon taking the next step, which was to register with the Ministry (Department) of Interior Affairs and open up a business file as a writer and lecturer, just about everyone we knew (non-Believers and Believers alike) tried to dissuade us from doing it.

In Israel the bureaucracy is so thick that it is necessary to hire professional lawyers and accountants to assist one with the paperwork. So now, with a "business" on our hands, not only would the Father have to supply what we needed for the month, but also the means to pay the various taxes.

The tax authorities already had an estimated income for these professions, and informed us how much we would have to pay for the first six months. We began to realize why people were trying to advise us against taking that route. However, we knew from the Word that we were to render to Caesar the things that are Caesar's, but to God the things that are His (reference Matthew 22:21).

I had another problem with this new profession, as my writing skills and ability to express myself through that medium were a two on a scale of one to ten.

I definitely needed a miracle. As a matter of fact, I even protested to my Heavenly Father, emphatically asking Him to supply the skills if He was indeed calling me to write. Although He didn't change my abilities, He did show me that my wife could be of help in that area.

During 1997 I taught in different places in Jerusalem and Ashkelon, I shared with some tour groups, and I led one of the home groups in the congregation. But as the end of August approached, and my last check arrived from the Ministry (Department) of Education, a very unsettling feeling began to race through my stomach. Then almost without warning, and to our amazement, during the month of September, Abba's paychecks began to arrive, and they always covered our expenses.

This was the case month by month. The month of November is especially memorable as it was then that we received a note from the bank warning us that we had gone over our allotted overdraft.

The four of us were standing in a circle in the living room, looking at this piece of paper, when the phone rang. It was from friends who had us teach in some courses in Jerusalem. They happened to be in our area and were asking if they could stop for a moment. When they arrived, they just handed us an envelope and left. Somehow we resumed our former position, and so, standing again in our little circle, we opened the envelope. To our amazement it was exactly the amount we needed to cover the overdraft.

That year was not an easy one, as we had to adjust to a new lifestyle of working together side by side every day. Our relationship had to take on a new dimension. New challenges occurred and we had to press on and into the Messiah for a lot of help.

For the children, it was a time of growing in faith. They were not quite teenagers then, and they had to pray and seek God for their needs, as well as to hear His voice as to what would be "affordable" (and therefore approved of by Him). They also had to learn about things that were not "affordable."

Many times I thought that our decision to follow this path might have been a mistake, but it was obvious that the Father was faithful to take care of us.

At about that time a visiting couple came into our lives and gave us a book about their life story. It was called *A Lifestyle of Light,* written by James M. Nesbit. It is a testimony of how the Father used this couple to "be about His business." It tells the story of how He took care of all their needs for twenty years or more. Reading it was very timely, as well as an incredible encouragement.

Finally, March of 1998 rolled around, and I had to give a final answer to the school as to whether I was returning the following year. Abba continued to impress on us that we were to carry on in this new "business." And that is what we did.

We have never regretted the decision we made and continue to be thankful to be working for a loving, faithful and merciful Heavenly Father.

"A man's heart plans his way, but the Lord directs his steps" (Proverbs16:9 NKJV).

## His Business

Over the years there was one question that puzzled me and was always at the forefront of my thoughts regarding the union of the "two sticks," or "trees," of Ezekiel 37:

*"How are these 'Two Houses' and their future reunion connected to God's Kingdom on earth?"*

Yeshua's disciples posed a similar question when they were on the Mount of Olives with their Master, just before His departure from this realm. They asked Him, "Lord, is it at this time You are restoring the kingdom to Israel?" (Acts 1:6).

What did Yeshua's followers mean by the term "restore"? Its very usage seems to indicate that God's Kingdom had been present in Israel sometime in the past.

One morning, while reading Acts 28:3 I suddenly realized that if I were to launch out in the "business" of the Gospel of the Kingdom, I too would have to believe and "be persuaded" concerning "the kingdom of God and Yeshua from both the Law of Moses and from the Prophets," just like those Jewish and non-Jewish residents of Rome two thousand years ago.

I would have to believe that what Paul taught as he was "explaining...by solemnly testifying about the kingdom of God, and trying to persuade...[his listeners] concerning Yeshua [Jesus] from both the Law of Moses and the Prophets..." (Acts 28:23).

*"In what way is the good news of God's Kingdom and His Messiah presented in the first five books of the Bible?"* I wondered to myself.

On that same day I also happened to read Psalm 145, where I encountered the words that made a marked impression on me: "Your kingdom is an everlasting kingdom, and Your dominion endures throughout all generations" (Verse 13).

If God's Kingdom had been "throughout all generations," then surely it must have been in the first one," I construed. So, turning the pages back to Genesis chapter one, I prayed, "Holy Spirit teach me."

Having read and studied the Bible over the years, I knew that the Holy Spirit could unearth new truths and revelations at any given moment. And that He actually exhorts us, "Call to Me and I will answer you, and I will tell you great and mighty things, which you do not know" (Jeremiah 33:3).

Was this the time for another such "illumination"?

In a matter of a few minutes of reading, one little word stood out to me. It impacted my understanding of the Scriptures from that point on. That word was the Hebrew verb *"r'du."* It is used in Geneses 1:26-28, and it means "to rule" or "have dominion."

It occurred to me that Adam, meaning both man and woman, were to be God's representative kings and priests over His creation. That is, they were to rule the "Kingdom of God" on earth.

However, because of the severed relationship of these first parents from their Creator, they needed a redeemer who would restore them back to Himself. Thus God's Word became the blue print for the restoration of His kingdom-rule-through-man over the creation.

As these seminal thoughts burgeoned, I began to understand God's statutes, ordinances, and laws in a new light: I saw them as part of Abba's Plan of Redemption.

He chose a firstborn (Abraham), to make a personal covenant with him and his descendants, and he destined them to become a nation of kings and priests, governing all nations in righteousness, justice and mercy.

Yet, because of man's inherent nature, this chosen firstborn nation also had to be redeemed. So the Sovereign Creator sent His Only Begotten Son to fulfill redemption's requirements, and thus to accomplish the restoration of His Kingdom to all Israel.

To His disciples' question, this Son of God, our Messiah, responded in the following manner: "It is not for you to know times or epochs which the Father fixed by His own authority; and you will receive power when the Holy Spirit has come upon you; and you shall be My witnesses both in Jerusalem, and in all Judea and Samaria, and even to the remotest part of the earth" (Acts 1:7-8).

In one breath the disciples' question was answered —and so was mine. They would be witnesses of the restoration of His Kingdom to Israel when the Holy Spirit would come upon them.

Some time later, Paul the Apostle, the Sent One, defined the nature of this Kingdom: "For the kingdom of God is not eating and drinking, but righteousness and peace and joy in the Holy Spirit" (Romans 14:17 NKJV).

Because I had also been filled with this same Spirit, I had to conclude that I too was now a witness of this same restoration.

Sharing this insight and awareness with others

became a passion that would lead and guide me into seeking further knowledge of our Lord and Savior Yeshua the Messiah.

It would motivate me to be about His business of restoring the Kingdom to all Israel—a restoration which will culminate in the two sticks (trees), Two Houses of Israel—Judah and Ephraim—coming back together under the rule of the Messiah King and High Priest.

Yeshua will not return until "the times of restoration of all things about which God spoke by the mouth of His holy prophets from ancient time" (Acts 3:21).

At this time, He is engaged in the process of gathering the second stick (or nation) of Joseph (Ephraim). He is doing this by His Spirit. He is restoring to the members of this nation their Hebraic roots. He is turning their hearts to their natural fathers, Abraham, Isaac, and Jacob just as promised in Malachi 4:6: "He will restore the hearts of the fathers to their children and the hearts of the children to their fathers."

This resurrection of these banished ones of Israel, from the valley of dry bones and out of the graves of non-existence, is just as important as the restoration of the stick of Judah back to the Land.

Ephraim, the rejected tribes, the orphans of Israel, must first know who they are as the second stick or nation, and then be joined to their brother Judah. This is not a political or religious move; it is a sovereign work of the Spirit of the living, covenant-keeping God of Abraham, Isaac and Jacob.

In 1983 the Spirit impressed upon me the reality of Ephraim being the *"m'lo haGoyim,"* the "fullness of the Gentiles."

Now, after twenty years of watching our God bringing them out of oblivion, Jacob's words, uttered on the day he crossed his hands and laid them upon the heads of Joseph's two sons, Ephraim and Menashe, are gaining increasing importance in the hearts of his seed: "The

God, before whom my fathers Abraham and Isaac walked, the God who has been my shepherd all my life to this day, the angel who has redeemed me from all evil, bless the lads and may my name live on in them, and the name of my fathers Abraham and Isaac; and may they grow into a multitude in the midst of the earth" (Genesis 48:15-16).

Our God has had four thousand years of sowing the scattered seed of our forefathers. Now is the time for their harvest.

Truly, the fields are ripe with the seed of the Patriarchs, Abraham, Isaac, and Israel. It is time for them to be gathered.

We must realize that the Word of the Lord is stamped into the lives of the Patriarchs and their progeny like a genetic code. This explains why so many feel a deep longing in their inner man to return to the Land, and upon arrival there exclaim, "I'm home! I'm home!"

I thank the Shepherd God of Israel daily for the privilege of being about His business of bringing the good news of the restoration of His Kingdom to both Houses of Israel.

The angel Gabriel said it all when the Father sent him to proclaim the good news to a Jewish virgin, "Behold, you will conceive in your womb and bear a son, and you shall name Him Yeshua [which means Salvation]. He will be great and will be called the Son of the Most High; and the Lord God will give Him the throne of His father David; and He will reign over the house of Jacob forever, and His kingdom will have no end" (Luke 1:31-33).

May it all be done to His glory and to the glory of His Son Yeshua.

May it be so in your life and in mine.

Amen!

Ephraim and Rimona
with Yonatan and Sehter-Hadar
Under their Olive Tree

# Return to the Land

## Who Is Israel? Past, Present, and Future by Batya Ruth Wootten The

scriptural answer to this provocative question is causing a stir in the Body of Messiah. It is sparking a reformation and inspiring Believers everywhere!

Who is Israel? Why do *you* need to know? The way you define Israel sets the course for your interpretation of Scripture. This popular book, now in its third edition, explains the truth about "both the houses of Israel" (Isaiah 8:14)—Ephraim and Judah. Reading it will help you to: Discover your Hebraic Heritage – Understand Israel and the Church – The Father's master plan for Israel. It will explain why you feel something is missing in your life – Why you have a love for Israel and Jewish people – And why you feel an urge to celebrate the feasts of Israel. Includes maps and charts. Paper, 288 pages $14.95    ISBN 1-886987-17-3

## Ephraim and Judah: Israel Revealed by Batya Ruth Wootten

Inexpensive. Succinct. Easy-to-read. This condensed overview of the material presented in the classic, *Who Is Israel?*, includes maps, charts, and lists. Like its parent, this book too is encouraging a reformation in the Body of Messiah. It quickly clarifies misconceptions about Israel's Twelve Tribes. It is an excellent tool that helps non-Jewish Believers see that they too are part of Israel. It also helps both the houses of Israel see how and where they fit into the Father's divine plan (Jeremiah 31:18-19; Ephesians 2:11-22; Isaiah 8:14).

This invaluable handout readily outlines the essence of the phenomenal truth of the two houses of Israel. Paper, 80 pages, $ 3.95    ISBN 1-886987-11-4

## Now in Spanish: ¿Quién es Israel? Based on an

earlier edition of *Who is Israel?*, this classic is also available in Spanish. 320 pages. $14.95    ISBN 1-886987-08-4

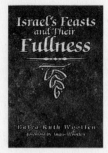

## Israel's Feasts and their Fullness

by Batya Wootten Liberating. Informative. Concise. At last, a book about the feasts especially for both the houses of Israel. Well researched, insightful, highly enjoyable work. Offers celebration suggestions that encourage us in the joy and freedom of the Messiah, yet show reverence for the accuracy of Scripture and due respect for Judaism's honorable truths. Addresses Shabbat and the seven feasts of Israel. Includes "Instruction Guides" for the Sabbath, Havdalah, and Passover, plus numerous charts, tables, and graphics. Batya continues in the style that has endeared her to so many of her readers as she encourages us to dance and sing and celebrate in the presence of the Almighty! Paper, 384 pages, $17.95 ISBN 1-886987-02-5

## Passover in all its Fullness

Offers the Passover related chapters from the above Feast book, plus helpful Passover Instruction Guides and traditional Messianic Jewish Pesach Haggadah. Explains the Four Pass-overs of Scripture, the meaning of First Fruits. An ideal gift at Passover celebrations. 96 pages, $4.95 ISBN 1-886987-15-7

## Mama's Torah: The Role of Women

by Batya Wootten The fresh ideas offered in this book about the restoration of women and Israel are compelling. Explains the God-ordained role of women and encourages us to release these vessels of mercy. Defines what it means to be a "help meet." Explains why women sometimes seem to be "against" their husbands. Delightfully depicts the roles of husband and wife. Lists women who were used in the Old and New Covenants and defines *how* they were used. Addresses Scriptures that have traditionally been used to hinder women in their walk. Reveals the Father's call to women in this hour. Includes study helps. Paper, 144 pages, $9.95 ISBN 1-886987-20-3

### Restoring Israel's Kingdom by
Angus Wootten As they stood on the Mount
of Olives, the last question Yeshua's disciples
asked of Him was,

*"Lord, is it at this time You are restoring
the kingdom to Israel?" (Acts 1:6).*

Yeshua told us to pray, "Your kingdom
come. Your will be done, on earth as it is in
heaven." He proclaimed "the gospel of the
kingdom," saying it must be "preached in the whole world as a
testimony to all the nations, and then the end will come"
(Matthew 6:10; 24:14).

Have we lost sight of the vision that once burned in the
hearts of His first disciples? Do we truly understand the gospel?
Do we have the same goal as that of the Messiah of Israel? This
inspiring book will help you to keep your eye on the goal.
Chapters include: Are You Prepared? – Learning the Lessons
of History – Who is a Jew? A Look at Israel's Bloodline – The
Way of the Gentiles – Ephraim, Once Again a Mighty Man –
The Jubilee Generation – Restoring The Kingdom To Israel –
The Messianic Vision – When Will Yeshua Return? – Preparing
For The Final Battle. Paper, 304 pages, $14.95 ISBN
1-886987-04-1

### Take Two Tablets Daily: The 10 Commandments and 613 Laws by
Angus Wootten Shows the laws of Moses to be
instructions given to help Israel be strong,
courageous, healthy, and blessed.

This handy guide lists the 613 laws, divided
into Mandatory Commandments and
Prohibitions (according to Jewish custom). It
also gives the Scripture verse(s) from which
each law is derived.

YHVH's Word is like medicinal ointment, and nothing is
more symbolic of His Word than the two tablets on which He
wrote His desires for us. Taken daily, these "Two Tablets" will
give us life more abundantly. This reference book should be in
every Believers library. It is a must read. 96 pages, $4.95
ISBN1-886987-06-8

# Return to the Land

## My Beloved's Israel by Gloria
Cavallaro Deepen your personal relation- ship with your Bridegroom. Embark on an intimate journey into the heart of our Heavenly Father. Experience a relationship with the Holy One of Israel like David described in his Psalms. Know an intimacy with the Bridegroom like that spoken of by Solomon in his Song of Songs.

Gloria chronicles her visions and dreams and interprets them in light of scriptural reflection. She concludes that Israel must be reunited if she is to be prepared for coming latter-day challenges. This personal journal exhorts and encourages intimacy with the Holy One. It helps prepare one's heart for the days ahead. Paper, 384 pages $16.95 SBN1-886987-05-X

## All Israel Dances Toward the
Tabernacle by Chester Anderson and Tina Clemens This inspiring book defines the dynamics of worship. It takes you beyond other worship books and answers many dance related questions: What is dance? – How did it originate? – What if I don't know how to dance? – Does something special happen in the heavenlies when we dance? – What attitude should be in our hearts when we are dancing and why? – Why do I feel so drawn to Hebraic dance? – Why has Davidic dance become so popular? – How does dance come into play in the restoration of both the houses of Israel?

This book will fill your heart with hope for the Glory that is soon to be upon us! It will set your feet a-dancin.'
Paper, 192 pages, $12.95 ISBN 1-886987-09-2

*Watch for more exciting titles from Key of David Publishing –*
*Working to "Unlock your future..."*

*Key of David, PO Box 700217, Saint Cloud, FL 34770*
*407 344-7700*

## Return to the Land: An Ephraimite's Journey Home by

Ephraim Frank As a new Believer, Ephraim could not explain what he felt burning in his soul. He only knew that he was being drawn, wooed by His God, and that he had gone on a tour that had forever changed his life...

From the farm lands of America to the Holy Land of Israel, this compelling auto-biography tells of a "stranger" who felt divinely drawn to both the Promised Land and the God of Abraham, Isaac, and Jacob. It tells of the birthing of a new and fresh move of the Holy One, while it gently reveals what the Father is doing in the earth today. It tells of the blessed redemption of the whole house of Israel. Paper, 240 pages, $12.95   ISBN 1-886987-18-1

## One Nation Under God by

Crystal Lenhart   Good News for our Children! This illustrated and fun book is written on a fifth grade level and will help you share your faith with your children. (It also can help parents better understand Israel.) This useful tool will help you teach your children in a family-oriented Bible study.   Great for home schooling and elementary adult studies. Features pages to color, lots of graphics, maps, and illustrations, plus easily understood lesson overviews and summaries.

Crystal writes, "The Bible speaks of one nation that was designed to be an example for all other nations. In Psalm 147, the Psalmist tells us that only this nation has been given God's Words and ordinances. The apostle Paul writes in Ephesians that every New Covenant Believer gains citizenship in this nation. What is this nation of the Bible? You guessed it, ISRAEL! Israel is Yahveh's nation, created to be a great nation with wise and understanding people, with a God who dwells among them and who has given them righteous laws to live by." Paper, Spiral Bound, 8x11, 76 pages, $12.00   ISBN 1-886987-16-5

*Distributed by:*

Messianic
Israel
Ministries

PO Box 3263
Lebanon, TN
37088

1 800 829-8777
www.mim.net